Biscuit the Dog

Finding the Heart of Servant Leadership

Tom Sorel

ISBN: 979-8-9942852-1-3 (Hardcover)
ISBN: 979-8-9942852-2-0 (ebook)
ISBN: 979-8-9942852-0-6 (Paperback)

Printed in the United States of America

Biscuit the Dog: Finding the Heart of Servant Leadership

Portions of this manuscript, including select illustrations, were developed with the assistance of artificial intelligence (AI) tools under the direction and authorship of Tom Sorel. All creative concepts, structure, imagery, and editorial decisions reflect the author's original work and intent.

Published by Daddy Boots Press

First Edition

Visit my website at www.tomsorel.com

Dedication

To Biscuit —

whose gentle presence showed us how to love, serve, and lead with joy, compassion, and a wagging tail.

2006–2022 — gone from our arms,
but forever guiding our hearts.

Acknowledgments

No book is created alone. This work grew from the conversations, quiet encouragement, and lived examples of so many who walked beside me.

To my wife Laurie and son Matt, thank you for your patience, laughter, and love. You gave me the space to write, to remember, and to honor Biscuit's spirit. I am grateful for every step we have shared.

To all the other dogs who entered my life, Rusty, Taffy, Frankie, and Allen, thank you. Each of you had a unique personality, yet each shared your love with me and made my life richer and more whole.

To the colleagues, friends, and leaders who lived these values long before I understood them, thank you for showing me what servant leadership looks like in motion. Your steady presence shaped the reflections in these pages more than you know.

And to everyone who welcomed Biscuit into their lives, whether for a moment or for many years, thank you. Her lessons live on because so many of you saw her heart.

"May you walk gently, listen deeply,
and lead with a heart of service,
just as Biscuit taught us to do."

With gratitude,
Tom

Table of Contents

About the Author, *Tom Sorel*

Tom Sorel grew up in a small town in upstate New York. He is the youngest of three siblings and spent his childhood playing in the woods with friends, enjoying his mother's home cooking, and tossing a baseball with his father in the backyard of their modest home. After graduating from a rural high school, he continued his education at the University at Buffalo, where he obtained a Bachelor of Science in civil engineering. He also earned an MBA from Thomas College in Maine.

Tom is a lifelong public servant whose leadership journey has been shaped more by people and community than by degrees or titles. Guided by deep humility and a belief that leadership begins with service, Tom has spent more than four decades helping organizations focus on people first, build trust, strengthen communities, and lift others along the way.

Over his career, Tom has held significant leadership roles in state and national transportation, including service as the Commissioner of the Minnesota Department of Transportation (MnDOT) and the Director of the North Dakota Department of Transportation (NDDOT). At both agencies, he led major initiatives centered on safety, collaboration, and culture change, most notably North Dakota's Vision Zero effort, which drove significant reductions in traffic fatalities by uniting state agencies around a shared mission that every life matters.

Prior to his state leadership roles, Tom served more than 30 years with the Federal Highway Administration, ultimately leading its St. Paul Division. He guided the U.S. Department of Transportation's intermodal team during the 2002 Olympic Winter Games in Salt Lake City, helping ensure safe and reliable mobility for millions of visitors from around the world.

Tom received a U.S. Presidential Honor for leading the local federal transportation response and recovery efforts following the catastrophic I-35W Bridge collapse in Minneapolis. His federal leadership contributed to the bridge being rebuilt and reopened in just 437 days, a milestone of collaboration, innovation, and resolve achieved with many state and local agencies. His servant leadership approach during that effort became the subject of a case study in *The Seven Pillars of Servant Leadership* by James Sipe and Don Frick.

Beyond his public service, Tom has helped shape industry and organizational cultures through key leadership positions in the private and not for profit sectors. In every role, he has worked to grow people and create environments where individuals feel valued, supported, and able to contribute their best.

Though his resume is rich with titles and recognitions, Tom measures his success in something simpler: whether people felt cared for, respected, and empowered along the way. He believes his greatest teachers were not found only in conference rooms or government buildings, but in relationships with colleagues, family, and, most unexpectedly, a gentle shelter dog named Biscuit.

It is through Biscuit's everyday wisdom, her joy, loyalty, courage, and quiet understanding, that Tom rediscovered the heart of servant leadership. Her example inspired this book, crafted to help others recognize the power of leading with love, presence, and purpose.

Tom continues to write, teach, speak, and mentor servant leaders everywhere. He lives in Minnesota with his loving wife Laurie, who holds him accountable for being a servant leader every day, as does his new best canine friend Allen, an energetic rescue who loves having his belly rubbed. His son Matthew lives close by with his amazing rescue dog, Frank.

Tom lives his life by a simple belief:
When we serve first, we lead best.

Foreword

I was newly retired when I first met Tom Sorel on a pickleball court in Oneonta, New York. Who would have known that our friendly pickleball matches would lead to wide-ranging conversations about our shared love of family and baseball? One day, our conversation turned to the subject of leadership. Once Tom and I started talking about leadership, we realized that we were very similar in our approach and beliefs about how to lead. Servant leadership was at the core of how both Tom and I lead.

Tom and I had very similar, yet diverse, leadership opportunities. Tom started out working for the federal government and, over time, served as the USDOT liaison for transportation at the 2002 Winter Olympic Games in Salt Lake City, Utah. In August of 2007, Tom was the lead local federal official in charge of the response to the I-35W Bridge collapse in Minneapolis, Minnesota. He later became the Commissioner of the Minnesota Department of Transportation and then took the same position working for the Governor of North Dakota.

I spent 36 years in the Air Force, and over that time led at the squadron, wing, and national level. I spent over 20 years flying and working in Antarctica with the 109th Airlift Wing, supporting the National Science Foundation's critical scientific research as well as its international collaboration mission. I was the deployment commander for the rescue of Dr. Jerri Nielsen from South Pole Station in Antarctica in October of 1998. In 2006, I was named Wing Commander of the 109th Airlift Wing. In 2010, I was promoted to Brigadier General and worked Hurricanes Irene and Sandy in New York City. In 2015, I was promoted to Major General and later appointed by the Governor of New York to his cabinet as the 53rd Adjutant General, in charge of the Army and Air National Guard.

Our similarities are many. We both grew up in small towns in upstate New York in the 1970s. Small-town living, strong families, and baseball shaped our early thoughts on leadership. We were long-time federal and state leaders, and we worked numerous disaster responses at the state and national level. We were called to lead through highly visible government responses and to follow the orders of those we worked for. We both worked at the cabinet level for our governors, and we both had numerous bosses over our careers who taught us how to lead and how not to lead.

It is very humbling for me to write the foreword for Biscuit the Dog: Finding the Heart of Servant Leadership. Whether we know it or not, we are all leaders, and we are all led. It doesn't matter if you lead one person or thousands; we can all benefit from learning how to treat each other by reading this book. There have been volumes of books written about leadership, but I have not read one like this. What Tom does in this book is genuinely fascinating. It reads as a story seen through the eyes of his dog, Biscuit. Each chapter is a page turner, starting with a Biscuit the Dog anecdote, followed by real-life leadership examples, and concluding with thoughtful reflections and thought-provoking questions. Once I started reading it, I couldn't put it down. Tom covers a wide range of topics that not only help you as a leader, but also strengthen all of your relationships, especially those with friends and family.

It is an honor to call Tom Sorel a friend, but more importantly, he is the epitome of a servant leader. Tom not only writes about servant leadership; he exemplifies it through his actions. My hope is that you will see Tom's thesis in this book, which is that real leaders serve those they are in charge of. They try to make lives better, listen, encourage, show up, stand up for others, and allow mistakes to become learning opportunities.

By Anthony P. German, USAF, Major General Retired

Understanding Servant Leadership: The Heart Behind the Story

The words you've just read in the foreword capture so much of what servant leadership represents. It's a way of living that has shaped my own journey and one that came to life most vividly through the quiet lessons of a dog named Biscuit.

Before we begin Biscuit's story, I want to pause and share what this book is really about, the heart of servant leadership. It's a phrase I've lived, studied, and tried to embody for years, yet I've come to see that it isn't a theory or a management style; it's a way of life.

Servant leadership begins not with a desire to lead, but with a desire to serve. It starts in the quiet conviction that we are here to make life better for others, to lift people up, to listen, to care, and to love without condition. The paradox is that through serving, we naturally begin to lead. And those we serve, in turn, will grow, thrive, and become leaders themselves.

I've witnessed this truth in boardrooms and construction sites, in classrooms and communities. But perhaps the purest example of servant leadership that I've ever seen has not come from books, but from a dog named Biscuit.

When Biscuit came into my life, she didn't have to earn trust or prove her worth. She led with presence, not position. She taught through example, not instruction. She lived every day as though her purpose was to bring comfort, connection, and joy to others. Over time, I began to realize that she was quietly teaching the same lessons that I had spent my entire career trying to share, the lessons of a servant leader.

The servant leadership framework I often revisit comes from The Seven Pillars of Servant Leadership, a book I had the privilege of contributing to while practicing its principles throughout my life. The Seven Pillars are being a person of character, putting people first, being a skilled communicator, a compassionate collaborator, a foresightful thinker, a systems thinker, and possessing moral authority. These pillars serve as a roadmap for leading with integrity and heart.

When I look back now, I see that Biscuit embodied each of these pillars in her own way.

1. Person of Character: She was faithful and consistent, even when no one was watching.
2. People First: She always sensed when someone needed her, giving her attention freely.
3. Skilled Communicator: With just a look, she expressed comfort, empathy, and understanding.
4. Compassionate Collaborator: Through a look, a nudge, or a playful stance, she worked with us, not for attention, but to bring us all together.
5. Foresight: She seemed to anticipate my needs before I even knew them and often showed up by my side.
6. Systems Thinker: She understood her place in the family "pack" and was often right in the middle, bringing balance to the family.

7. Moral Authority: Through her quiet example, she earned respect, trust, and love from all those who were lucky to meet her.

Biscuit reminded me that servant leadership isn't about striving to check boxes or follow frameworks; it's about living with purpose and humility every day. The framework gives voice to something much deeper, the human, and sometimes canine, instinct to care for others.

As you read this book, I hope you'll see that servant leadership isn't limited to titles or organizations. It exists in families, friendships, and communities, anywhere hearts connect and compassion leads the way. My hope is that Biscuit's story helps you see the servant leader already within you, the part of you that listens, gives, forgives, and leads through love.

So, as we begin this journey together, open your heart to the lessons of an extraordinary teacher in a furry body, a dog who found joy in serving and, in doing so, revealed the very heart of servant leadership.

"Servant leadership begins not with the desire to lead, but with the desire to love."

A Note Before We Begin

Tom Sorel is a storyteller at heart.

He has spent a lifetime listening closely to the quiet lessons found in everyday life, in workplaces and neighborhoods, during long walks, and in small moments of connection. His career in public service and transportation leadership taught him that the best guidance rarely comes from titles or authority, but from kindness, curiosity, and a willingness to serve.

One of his greatest teachers was Biscuit, a rescue dog with a gentle spirit and a gift for seeing people beyond their roles. Through her presence, Tom learned that leadership begins not with directing others, but with caring for them; not with ambition, but with humility and love.

Tom shares these stories in hopes that each reader will notice the wisdom already present in their own lives, in the companions who walk beside them, the people who encourage them, and the moments that invite them to slow down, listen deeply, and lead with heart.

Chapter 1

A New Beginning, Discovering Servant Leadership

"Dogs have a way of finding the people who need them, filling in emptiness we don't even know we have."
— *Thom Jones*

When I first met Biscuit, it felt ordinary, until it wasn't. She was a rescue, gentle yet cautious, with eyes that held a quiet wisdom. I didn't know it then, but this four-legged companion would lead me into a new understanding of leadership, not through words, but through the quiet power of presence.

I felt an immediate connection the moment we locked eyes. Somehow, I knew she would have a profound impact on my life. I didn't even know what kind of dog she was; the shelter listed her as a terrier mix. None of that mattered. What mattered was her spirit, a beautiful blend of strength and gentleness that drew me in.

That first day wasn't perfect. There were nervous whimpers, hesitant steps, and moments of uncertainty as she explored an unfamiliar world. Yet there was something unmistakable about her presence, a calm patience that seemed to whisper, *"It's okay. We'll figure this out together."* It was as if she already understood what it meant to serve, before she ever learned to obey.

In those early days, I was struck by her consistency. She wasn't loud or demanding; she simply showed up, at the door when I came home, beside me when I read, and always, without fail, ready for a walk when she heard the leash jingle. Biscuit loved her walks. She'd glance back every few steps, making sure I was still there. That shared comfort was special, an unwritten agreement that we were in this together.

During this time in my life, I was facing complex leadership challenges, difficult decisions, shifting expectations, and the weight of public service. I was searching for a leadership approach that could steady both me and those I served. I'd read all the popular leadership books, yet something still felt incomplete. I didn't need more strategy; I needed grounding.

In Biscuit, I found a teacher.

Her way of moving through the world, steady, observant, and unshaken, reminded me that leadership begins with *being*. Then it clicked: the qualities I saw in her, patience, humility, and presence, were the very qualities of a servant leader. That realization changed everything.

One evening, after a particularly hard day, I sat in my car questioning my ability to lead. The meetings that afternoon had been rough, and criticism came easily. I felt defeated. Before I could gather the strength to go inside, Biscuit bounded out to greet me. She placed her paws gently on my shoulders and gave me her familiar nose nuzzle. In that instant, all the self-doubt melted away. She didn't need me to be perfect, just *present*. That small act of love became our nightly ritual, reminding me that the best leaders bring peace simply by showing up.

That was the true beginning of my journey with servant leadership.

⬭ Personal Reflection

Looking back, I see how Biscuit's quiet arrival mirrored the start of every leadership role in my life. We step into new roles uncertain of ourselves, testing the ground beneath our feet. But when we lead with humility, patience, and genuine care, we build trust that lasts. Biscuit became my daily reminder that servant leadership doesn't begin with doing; it begins with *being*.

Her steady loyalty taught me that presence alone can transform relationships. I learned that as a leader, I didn't have to fix everything; I just had to *show up*. That simple act of showing up opened the space for others to grow.

In my years leading two Departments of Transportation, I carried that lesson forward. Being present meant being accessible, listening to employees, legislators, and citizens with openness and respect. I made it a point to reach out on birthdays and celebrate milestones, simple gestures that said, *"You matter."* In time, that practice built stronger teams and elicited better solutions because people believed that they mattered. They also saw this leadership style of being present modeled by their top leaders, giving them permission to do the same.

I also came to understand the importance of articulating my leadership philosophy. After studying the academic side of servant leadership, I realized that true service flows from the heart. I invited my employees to explore this approach with me, never mandating it, only modeling it. At nearly every meeting, I wove in the essence of *servant leadership* and shared what the principles meant in practice.

One video I often played for employees was *"To a Child, Love Is Spelled T-I-M-E"* by Lance Wubbels and Mac Anderson. In it, a father cleaning his attic finds his and his son's journals describing a fishing trip they once took together. The father's entry calls it a wasted day because the fish weren't biting. His son's entry says it was the best day of his life. That story became a lasting reminder that our presence may seem small to us, but it can mean everything to someone else.

All these experiences solidified what Biscuit had taught me from the beginning, that real servant leadership comes from the heart and shows up in every situation.

 ## Closing Reflection

Every beginning carries both hope and hesitation. Biscuit's arrival reminded me that leadership doesn't start with grand gestures; it begins with humility and trust. Her gentle presence invited connection without demand, showing that the most powerful leadership is grounded in authenticity.

In her eyes, love was given unconditionally. Each greeting, each gentle nudge, and each quiet moment by my side spoke the same message, *you matter*. That is the heart of servant leadership, seeing others not as tasks to manage, but as people to care for.

Biscuit's example invites us to start right where we are, with the people beside us, leading with humility. It's not the size of the stage that defines a servant leader, but the size of the heart.

May we all lead with that same spirit, with love, being present, being faithful, and with quiet humility that never runs out.

 ## Pawprint Practice

Pause and Reflect: Intentionally notice one person you might normally overlook. Offer them your full attention through a greeting, question, or simple acknowledgment. Observe how that small act of presence changes the interaction.

Notice and Name: Think about the "Biscuit moments" in your own life, times when quiet love, patience, or encouragement made a difference. How might those moments shape your understanding of leadership?

Serve Intentionally: Identify one opportunity this week to lead through service, to offer help, understanding, or gratitude without being asked.

Listen Inwardly: Servant leadership begins with self-awareness. Ask yourself, how can I bring more humility, empathy, or presence into my leadership today?

Carry It Forward: Leadership doesn't begin when others notice you; it begins quietly when you start noticing others.

"The journey to becoming a servant leader begins not with ambition, but with awareness, the moment you realize that leadership is not about you, but about intentionally building up others."

Chapter 2

Small Acts, Big Heart:
The Power of Kindness

"The world would be a nicer place if everyone had the ability to love as unconditionally as a dog."
— *M.K. Clinton*

Biscuit never chased applause. She didn't need to be the center of attention. Yet time after time, she gave kindness quietly, without fanfare. She had a way of noticing the small needs around her and meeting them without hesitation, a gentle nudge when someone was sad, or a tail wag when spirits were low. These small acts spoke volumes.

There was something deeply moving about the way she saw people, not just with her eyes, but with her heart. I once watched her approach a crying little boy who was sitting alone in the park. The boy couldn't find his mom. Biscuit didn't bark or seek attention. She simply sat beside the boy, still and patient. After a moment, the mom showed up, relieved. She gently hugged Biscuit, knowing that the comfort Biscuit gave her son was just what was needed at that time.

Biscuit's kindness was contagious. On the side of our house was a gently sloping hill that became known as "Biscuit Hill" to all the neighbors.

It was her sanctuary, the place she retreated to on breezy summer days or during the hush of a snowfall. Over time, she buried little treasures there: old bones, hats, socks, and shoes. Neighbors would often stop by and find her lounging in the grass, wagging her tail as if welcoming them into her peaceful kingdom. They always walked away smiling. The same was true of other dogs who visited her on the hill. Some would play; others would help themselves to one of her buried bones. Biscuit never minded. Her generosity was effortless.

One frosty morning, I watched her walking across Biscuit Hill, her breath rising in soft clouds. A neighbor who had recently lost her husband approached from the path below. Without hesitation, Biscuit trotted to her, sat quietly at her feet, and looked up with those calm, knowing eyes. No bark, no demand, just presence. The woman knelt, tears filling her eyes, and whispered, "She remembers."

In a world obsessed with productivity and speed, leadership often becomes a race. But Biscuit reminded me that leadership is sometimes about slowing down, making room for others to be seen, heard, and acknowledged. That isn't just kindness, it's strength.

There's courage in choosing kindness, especially when it's inconvenient. I remember one day when everything felt rushed with deadlines, phone calls, and endless decisions. In the middle of the chaos, I noticed Biscuit sitting patiently by the door, waiting for me to take a break. It was not a convenient time for me. She didn't demand that I take a break, but she offered it. When I finally sat beside her, her calm presence helped me breathe again. Her patience was the kindness I didn't know I needed.

Servant leadership isn't about grand gestures. Sometimes, it's a wag of the tail, a listening ear, or a willingness to stay beside someone until they feel whole again. Biscuit taught me that kindness becomes a quiet form of leadership that transforms everything it touches.

💭 Personal Reflection

Biscuit's example of everyday kindness shaped the way I approached leadership in both my personal and professional life. I learned that kindness influences everything; it creates space for joy, healing, and connection. Professionally, I discovered that a culture of kindness can change an organization. It builds trust, strengthens morale, and encourages people to bring their best selves to work every day.

At MnDOT, I saw firsthand how kindness could become a leadership model. Although leadership models oftentimes come from the top, the talented people I surrounded myself with were leaders who naturally embodied kindness. When people see kindness modeled in their leaders, they feel empowered to extend kindness themselves. It doesn't have to be scripted or formal; it flows naturally when servant leadership is alive within a culture.

Some view kindness in leadership as weakness, but I've found it to be one of the greatest strengths. Being kind doesn't mean avoiding accountability or hard decisions; it means leading with empathy while pursuing excellence. It is about balancing firmness with grace, clarity, and compassion.

After the tragic collapse of the I-35W bridge in Minneapolis, Minnesota, kindness became our compass. As MnDOT Commissioner, I knew we had to rebuild not only infrastructure but public trust and confidence. I decided to try something new and create an external ombudsman to interact with the public as a way to manage conflict. The perfect person for this role, that I knew had a kind heart, was Deb Ledvina. Deb was seen as a servant leader by those who worked for her, and I knew she would be very successful in using her kindness with the public in situations that would require listening, empathy, and a kind heart.

Although Deb could have embraced this role just to resolve issues, instead she went beyond expectations and tapped into her kindness to serve people who became disenchanted with the Department. Deb's compassion became a bridge between the agency and those who had lost faith in MnDOT.

Within a short period of time, we recaptured the public's trust, and I believe servant leadership through the power of kindness played a key role. Deb's leadership, and her own kindness, was just outstanding. Her servant leader heart helped turn community outrage into common understanding.

Within the agency, kindness became our rallying force. We rebuilt morale not with slogans, but with small, human gestures: handwritten notes, open communication, unhurried conversations, and many listening opportunities. For people to talk and be heard, I invited every employee to share their story about the collapse, their fears, and their hopes for the future, and many did. In responding, I often wrote about "hope," and shared a passage from Margaret Wheatley's *Leadership and the New Science*:

"Dark times are normal to life; there's nothing wrong with us when we periodically plunge into the abyss."

We had indeed fallen into an abyss, but through hope and kindness, we climbed back out together. The resilience and compassion that emerged during this transformation reminded me so much of Biscuit's manner: gentle, steady, and faithful even in times of adversity.

During this time, I shared a short but powerful video called *Life Vest Inside: Kindness Boomerang*, created by Orly Wahba, a national speaker and founder of the nonprofit Life Vest Inside. The film captures how simple acts of kindness ripple outward, multiplying far beyond the original gesture. The message became a touchstone for us after the bridge collapse, reminding us that kindness is not just sentimental, but a practical way to rebuild trust, restore hope, and reconnect with one another. I returned to it often, using it to encourage our teams and our community to believe that every small act mattered, because it did.

Creating a culture of kindness, internally and externally, proved to be one of the most powerful leadership tools of all. It reminded us that servant leadership is not just a philosophy; its kindness expressed through daily actions.

 Closing Reflection — Small Acts, Big Heart

In a world that often measures success by speed and scale, kindness may seem small. Yet it is those quiet, consistent gestures that change the atmosphere around us. Biscuit showed that love expressed through small acts builds trust, heals hearts, and reminds people that they matter.

Biscuit's gentle spirit reminds us that kindness isn't weakness, its courage wrapped in compassion. It takes strength to pause, to notice, and to respond with love and kindness when it would be easier to turn away.

As servant leaders, our influence grows not from grand gestures but from the grace we extend in ordinary moments. Each smile, each word of encouragement, each patient pause becomes a ripple that spreads far beyond our view.

Biscuit's life was a collection of those ripples, a steady stream of compassion that continues to flow long after she's gone. She showed that you don't need power or position to change the world, you just need the courage to care.

Let kindness be your legacy, steady, quiet, and full of heart. Like Biscuit, lead with compassion so genuine that others feel lighter simply because you were there.

🐾 Pawprint Practice — Living with a Kind Heart

Pause and Reflect: Identify a person on your team or in your personal life who carries an unseen burden. Offer a small act of support that lightens their load without drawing attention to yourself.

Act with Intention: This week, look for opportunities to lead through small, quiet acts of kindness: a note of encouragement, an unexpected thank-you, or a moment of genuine listening.

Model Biscuit's Way: Notice how Biscuit never sought praise. She led through presence and care. Ask yourself: *Am I leading to be noticed, or to nurture others?*

Practice Generosity of Spirit: Kindness is more than behavior, it's a posture of the heart. Show grace in a difficult conversation or patience when pressure mounts.

Encourage Others: Recognize and celebrate acts of kindness in those around you. By doing so, you multiply its reach and strengthen the culture of compassion in your workplace, home, and community.

"Kindness is the language of servant leadership, quiet, powerful, and deeply human."

Chapter 3

Listening and Loyalty: Building Trust

"Dogs do speak, but only to those who know how to listen."
— *Orhan Pamuk*

Trust isn't built in declarations or job titles. It grows quietly, moment by moment, through presence, consistency, and care. Biscuit, in her humble and faithful way, was one of the finest listeners I've ever known. She didn't interrupt, judge, or try to fix anything. She simply stayed, grounded, calm, and attentive. In that stillness, I often found understanding that words could never provide.

Biscuit taught me that listening isn't about hearing sounds, it's about sensing what someone is feeling. She could tell when I was weary, anxious, or discouraged long before I said a word. Her head would tilt, her eyes would soften, and she'd sit beside me until the moment passed. She didn't demand that I explain myself, she just offered presence, and somehow that was enough.

When I came home after long days, especially during challenging times in public service, Biscuit's greeting never wavered. Her tail would drum a happy rhythm against the couch, her eyes sparkling with recognition. She'd follow me from room to room, not seeking attention, but offering connection. Once I sat down, she'd roll onto her back, trusting and relaxed, waiting for a familiar belly rub. That simple ritual grounded me in ways no meeting or plan ever could.

One morning stands out vividly in my memory. I had a high-stakes meeting with political leaders, the kind that demanded careful words and tested patience. Before leaving, I bent down, hugged Biscuit, and whispered, "I'll be back later." She looked up at me with steady eyes, full of quiet trust. That calm stayed with me. During the meeting, as tension rose, I pictured Biscuit's face, her loyalty, her stillness, her belief that connection outlasts conflict. It helped me stay grounded, composed, and true to myself. And when I returned home that evening, there she was, waiting, tail wagging, as if to say, *"You did fine."*

That's what trust looks like. It doesn't question your worth when things go wrong. It doesn't vanish when times are tough. It waits. It believes. It stays. Biscuit never missed her chance to show up. She was there even when it wasn't convenient, even when no one noticed.

In organizations, results often dominate our measures of success: numbers, milestones, and deliverables. But what if we measured reliability instead? What if the most trusted leaders were those who consistently showed up, calm, present, and loyal? Biscuit's kind of loyalty wasn't earned through obedience, it was mutual, built on respect and relationship.

Within the agencies I led, that mindset became a living practice. When leaders model reliability, when they truly listen, when their intent is pure, when their competence is evident, and when they follow through, trust grows naturally. People begin to feel seen, valued, and empowered. Soon, everyone becomes a leader in their own right, regardless of title or role.

That's how we rebuilt confidence in our organizations, not by command, but by consistency. Like Biscuit's gentle presence, trust spread one relationship at a time, one conversation at a time. The result wasn't just higher morale, it was a shared sense of purpose rooted in respect and caring.

When I picture Biscuit waiting by the door, patient and certain, I see the embodiment of trustworthy leadership. She didn't have to say a word to remind me what mattered most: be reliable, stay present, and lead with loyalty.

💭 Personal Reflection

Feeling Biscuit's loyal presence was an invaluable lesson I learned as I sought to cultivate trust in the organizations I led. When I became Commissioner of the Minnesota Department of Transportation and later Director of the North Dakota Department of Transportation, I was seen by many as an outsider. These were large state agencies, with

5,000 and 1,000 employees respectively, and while some people offered trust based on title, for most, trust had to be earned.

That's when I embraced Stephen M. R. Covey's *The Speed of Trust*. It gave language to what Biscuit had already modeled: that trust is built through consistent credibility — integrity, intent, capability, and results. Biscuit embodied all four. She was congruent, selfless, capable in her purpose, and unfailingly faithful to her quiet promise to be there.

Since political appointments often last only as long as the governor's term, building trust quickly is vital. Covey's "Four Cores of Credibility of Trust" became my leadership compass:

1. Integrity: Are you congruent?
2. Intent: What is your agenda?
3. Capabilities: Are you relevant?
4. Results: What's your track record?

To me, these principles meant living with integrity, maintaining positive intent, demonstrating competence, and keeping my word. As a servant leader, they became the foundation for every interaction with my employees and partners.

These same principles helped our agencies build external trust as well. As employees were empowered to demonstrate their own integrity and skill, trust grew organically, within teams and beyond. The more employees led through service, the more the agencies flourished. Though I held the formal title of leader, it became clear that *everyone* was a leader. Once that truth took hold, we served one another toward a common vision.

Trust, once earned, must be continually renewed. Biscuit's daily loyalty reminded me that it's not a one-time achievement, but an ongoing choice. You show up every day. You listen again. You care again. That's how trust endures, and how servant leadership takes hold.

Building and maintaining trust is sacred work. Once lost, it's difficult to regain. Biscuit's steady presence and unwavering faithfulness became part of who I am as a leader, and a reminder that consistency, humility, and love build bridges no title ever could.

✑ Closing Reflection — Listening and Loyalty: Building Trust

Trust is the foundation of every healthy relationship and effective team. It doesn't come with titles or authority, it's earned through presence, authenticity, and time.

Trust lives in the quiet spaces, the pauses between words, the moments when we listen instead of react. Biscuit never hurried or interrupted. Her loyalty was her language.

Her trust was unwavering because it was mutual. She didn't demand perfection, she simply believed in consistency. Through her, I learned that trust is not born out of control, but of confidence, the kind that grows when people know they are seen, heard, and valued.

In leadership, trust is both fragile and sacred. Once broken, it takes humility, courage, and kindness to rebuild. But each time we listen with empathy, honor our word, and stay steady through challenge, we rebuild that bridge a little stronger.

Let your leadership be like Biscuit's, steady in storms, gentle in conflict, and faithful through change. In that constancy, others will find the courage to trust, and in that trust, your leadership will truly take root.

Pause and Reflect: Look for opportunities when you can speak last in a team or group setting. Let others be fully heard before offering your perspective.

Listen with Intention: In your next individual conversation, listen not to reply, but to understand. Silence can be the most powerful tool for connection.

Show Up Reliably: Identify one relationship where you can show up more consistently this week. Send a message: "You can count on me."

Model Biscuit's Loyalty: Be emotionally present for someone today. You don't need to fix their problem, just stay close.

Rebuild When Needed: If trust has been strained, take the first step toward repair. Apologize sincerely, recommit to consistency, and rebuild through action.

"Trust isn't built through grand gestures, but through faithful presence, one quiet act of listening, one moment of staying true."

Chapter 4

Humility and Compassion: Putting Others First

"Be the person your dog thinks you are."
— *C.J. Frick*

Biscuit never acted like the world revolved around her. In truth, she had a gift for making everyone around her feel as if they were the most important person in the room. Her humility was not the absence of confidence, it was the presence of grace. She didn't need to be seen to feel fulfilled. Her joy came from giving attention, not seeking it.

There's a kind of leadership that doesn't roar for attention or demand the spotlight. It leads quietly, grounded in empathy and awareness. Biscuit lived that kind of leadership naturally. She sensed emotion before words could describe it. When someone was grieving or hurting, she would simply arrive, resting her head gently in their lap until peace began to return. When our son wrestled with disappointment or confusion, Biscuit was always close by, her calm presence offering comfort that no explanation could match.

Humility, I've come to believe, is knowing when it's not about you. Biscuit modeled this in every interaction. Even when others were distracted or distant, she remained present, not because she needed acknowledgment, but because she cared. Her leadership was invisible in the best possible way. It wasn't about control, but contribution.

Compassion, too, is often misunderstood. It's not softness or weakness, it's courage wrapped in kindness. It's the strength to stand beside others in their moments of pain, without judgment or superiority. Biscuit's compassion had no conditions. She gave her love freely, never asking who "deserved" it. Whether it was a child tugging her tail, a neighbor passing by, or a stranger who needed a smile, she responded the same way, with warmth and trust.

Her simple acts of connection became bridges between people. Biscuit had a way of making every encounter feel significant. She reminded me that leadership isn't about standing above others, it's about walking beside them. Her example became my compass for true servant leadership: seeing others first, listening with empathy, and acting with humility.

One image stays with me: Biscuit lying beside my son Matthew on the porch, their heads resting close together, breathing in rhythm. Nothing needed to be said. That silent companionship was enough. Compassion doesn't always need words, sometimes the quiet act of simply being present says everything.

True humility and compassion, when lived out, change the way people relate to one another. Humility and compassion create a culture of belonging. In leadership, they build trust that no policy or title ever could. When we lead with humility, we make room for others to shine. When we act from compassion, we remind people they matter.

Biscuit didn't just demonstrate these values, she invited everyone around her to live them too. Her presence softened hearts, opened conversations, and created moments of healing. Her legacy is a reminder that humility and compassion are not signs of passivity, they are the foundations of authentic strength.

In a world that often celebrates pride and position, Biscuit's quiet example remains a gentle truth, that the leaders who lead with humility and compassion and who put others first leave the deepest pawprints.

◯ Personal Reflection

Watching Biscuit live out compassion and humility was grounding. These qualities lie at the very core of servant leadership, and when lived authentically, they draw others in. Without them, people withdraw. Humility opens the mind to new ideas without preconceived notions, and though it's sometimes mistaken for weakness, over time it proves to be an extraordinary strength. It fosters empowerment, and it's contagious.

I saw this most clearly through people like Celine Carpenter, my executive assistant at MnDOT. Celine was a remarkable servant leader whose compassion and humility showed every day. She understood MnDOT's mission deeply and became a trusted resource for employees across all levels. During her busy days, it wasn't unusual to see someone in her office, seeking clarity, reassurance, or simply her steady presence.

People would often turn to Celine when they were struggling. She helped without judgment, always with warmth. Once, a colleague felt frustrated and unsure of her supervisor's expectations. Celine, who knew both well, mediated their conversation with such empathy that it transformed misunderstanding into mutual respect. Her laughter, kindness, and calm humility became a steady current that connected people across the agency. People were naturally drawn to her because she put them first.

Celine's example reminded me that titles never determine a person's capacity to lead, character does. Time after time throughout my career,

I saw people with humility and compassion emerge as extraordinary servant leaders, regardless of their formal authority.

Two such people were Jeff Ostrom and Phil Barnes, whom I met early in their public service journeys. Jeff worked in the Governor's Office of Constituent Services, and Phil was just beginning his path after completing the Federal Highway Administration's Training Program. Even then, I sensed something distinctly special in both of these fine men. Their approach to their work wasn't about ambition or recognition; it was about helping others succeed.

That alignment with servant leadership drew me to both men. I invited them to collaborate with me across several organizations over the years because I believed deeply in their potential to lead with heart.

I intentionally placed them in situations that stretched them, moments that asked them to step beyond what felt comfortable. They embraced those challenges, not because they sought credit, but because they truly wanted to make a difference. Along the way, I introduced them to leaders at state and national levels who could further expand their thinking and networks. Watching them absorb those experiences with quiet humility affirmed what I already knew: these men possessed the character of true servant leaders.

Today, both Jeff and Phil are remarkable leaders in their own right, professionally and within their families. Their success brings me great joy, not because of what they've accomplished, but because they chose to cultivate a life rooted in service to others.

What I learned most from mentoring Jeff and Phil was this: As servant leaders, part of our responsibility is knowing when to guide and when to release.

At a certain point, they didn't need my direction, they simply needed space to grow. And like Biscuit, who quietly encouraged without demanding attention, I realized that true leadership often means stepping back so others can blossom.

I'm proud of them, not just for what they've achieved, but for who they've become. Our relationship evolved from mentoring to mutual learning, friendship, and deep respect. It is one of the greatest gifts of my career.

History's most respected leaders often share this same quiet strength. They may not always occupy the spotlight, but those around them recognize their authenticity. Their humility and compassion become magnets, drawing in trust, talent, and collaboration.

In our personal lives, too, we are naturally drawn to people who are humble and kind. Like Biscuit, they put their own self-interest aside, creating space for others to thrive. Humility and compassion don't diminish our power, they deepen it. They allow us to serve in ways that uplift rather than overshadow.

Biscuit didn't just model humility and compassion, she invited everyone near her to live with humility and compassion.

꩜ Closing Reflection — The Quiet Strength of Servant Leadership

Humility and compassion are the twin lights of servant leadership, one grounds us, the other guides us. Biscuit lived both with quiet grace. She never sought the spotlight, yet her presence warmed every room she entered. Her strength came not from dominance, but from gentleness.

Humility invites connection, compassion sustains it. Together, they form the heartbeat of servant leadership.

Biscuit approached every person without judgment, whether joyful, hurting, or uncertain, and offered her presence as a gift. Her power was not in commanding attention but in showing care. Through her, I learned that the strongest leaders are often the quietest ones, those who choose listening over lecturing and understanding over proving.

Humility asks us to lead with open hands instead of clenched fists, to serve without needing credit, and to care without expectation. Compassion calls us to see beyond ourselves, to notice the needs, fears, and hopes of others, and respond with empathy. Biscuit showed that you don't need authority to make a lasting difference. Sometimes the smallest kindness, the softest gesture, or the simplest act of presence can heal more than words ever could.

May you find the courage to serve in ways that go unseen, to listen when it's inconvenient, and to respond to others' pain with kindness instead of defense. In doing so, you'll discover what Biscuit knew instinctively, that the heart of leadership is love, humble, gentle, and enduring.

🐾 Pawprint Practice — Choosing Humility, Living Compassion

Pause and Reflect: In one decision this week, intentionally choose what benefits someone else, not what elevates you. Observe what that shift changes.

Lead by Lowering: True humility doesn't mean thinking less of yourself; it means thinking of yourself less often. Find one way to elevate someone else this week through encouragement, opportunity, or gratitude.

Practice Compassion in Action: Notice where someone around you may be struggling silently. Offer your support, not with advice or judgment, but with patient presence.

Learn from Biscuit: Biscuit's compassion was quiet but constant. She didn't seek recognition, only connection. How might you lead with that same quiet confidence?

Reflect on Leadership: Ask yourself: *Do I lead to be right, or to make things right?* The answer reveals whether humility is guiding your actions.

Grow Together: Compassion deepens trust. Share a story of someone who showed you grace, and let that memory inspire you to do the same for others.

"Compassion and humility are not signs of weakness, they are the soil where true strength and trust take root."

Chapter 5

The Strength of Vulnerability: Accepting Support as a Servant Leader

"Petting, scratching, and cuddling a dog can be as soothing to the mind and heart as deep meditation, and almost as good for the soul as prayer."
— Dean Koontz

Biscuit was brave, but she had her fears. Every Fourth of July, the sharp crackle of fireworks sent her trembling. Her confident posture melted into anxiety, her calm demeanor turned restless and unsure. Her wide eyes darted nervously, her body shaking so hard I could feel it through my arms. My first instinct was to make it stop, but I knew the only thing to do was to wait it out, together.

And something beautiful happened in those moments. Biscuit allowed herself to be vulnerable. She leaned into comfort instead of resisting it. I would lie with her for hours, wherever she felt safe: on the floor, in a corner, on the couch, or on the bed. Wrapped in a heavy blanket, her head buried against my chest, she let me carry some of the weight of her fear. She didn't need to be strong all the time, and she trusted me enough to be vulnerable.

Even after the fireworks ended, it took time for her to believe the noise was gone. Once her trembling eased, we'd sit side by side, and I'd offer her a favorite treat. She would look at me with eyes that seemed to say, "*Thank you.*" The next belly rub wasn't about fear anymore, it was about openness and love.

As humans, we are often taught that leaders must be stoic, that showing vulnerability is a weakness. But Biscuit showed me something far more powerful: vulnerability is an invitation for connection. Her openness created space for love, care, and trust.

Servant leadership isn't about being impenetrable, it's about being real. It's knowing when to ask for help, when to admit fear, and when to say, "I can't do this alone." Biscuit never asked out loud, but in the way she leaned into vulnerability, she gave me permission to do the same.

Vulnerability doesn't make us lesser leaders, it makes us human. Biscuit's trembling body in my arms wasn't weakness; it was a powerful act of trust. In holding her, I learned that accepting help isn't a burden to others, it's a gift.

⟁ Personal Reflection

Biscuit's vulnerability was another awakening in my servant leadership journey. Her willingness to accept comfort is a lesson every servant leader should embrace.

I think of Holly Kostrzewski, whom I first met while we both worked at MnDOT. As the Northwest Minnesota *Towards Zero Deaths* (TZD) Regional Director, Holly worked with federal, state, local, and tribal leaders to reduce traffic fatalities. She worked with diverse groups of people who would always follow her. Holly did a remarkable job in this role, but her life story is where the true strength of vulnerability shines.

At eighteen, Holly sustained a traumatic brain injury in a car crash. She had to relearn nearly everything: walking, talking, even basic daily routines. At this most vulnerable point in her life, she learned to accept help from others. Rather than give in to despair, she thrived on that support and became a keynote speaker on traumatic brain injury (TBI), traveling the world to share her story.

Holly still has challenges, and her family has helped her with them, but her resilience continues to inspire. Her strength came to the forefront when this past year she went to the site of her crash and was able to witness the groundbreaking of a traffic safety improvement project. For Holly, this brought her story full circle as she saw important safety measures put in place to help others.

Holly often says everyone has a *"junk drawer"* inside, a place where unsorted struggles are stored. As a self-proclaimed *Ambassador of Hope,* she helps others sort through those drawers and embrace their vulnerabilities. Holly's vulnerability has helped make her into the true servant leader she is today.

Just as Biscuit leaned into comfort instead of resisting it, Holly embraced the support she needed to rebuild her life. Her journey reminded me again and again that vulnerability isn't the absence of strength, it's what refines it. When we show up authentically with vulnerability, we give others permission to do the same. Vulnerability isn't the end of strength, it's the beginning of it.

In my own leadership roles, I tried to model that same honesty and openness. Saying "I don't know, but I will find out" is not weakness, it's wisdom. It shows humility and a commitment to finding the right path forward.

After the collapse of the I-35W bridge, there were countless questions we couldn't yet answer until investigations were complete. That was okay. What mattered was being transparent and vulnerable with the public and showing our commitment to ensuring it never happened again.

I'll never forget being at the National Transportation Safety Board (NTSB) hearing when the collapse investigation results were released. During a break, a small group of us gathered in a corner and suddenly began to cry. The raw grief we felt for the victims, families, and the tragedy of that day overwhelmed us. In that moment, our vulnerability united us, and that's what servant leaders do.

Too often, people avoid vulnerability out of fear, often rooted in past experiences or trauma. But embracing it opens the door to resilience, trust, and genuine connection. As Biscuit taught me, vulnerability is strength. During the times she feared the sound of fireworks, she stayed close, accepting comfort by my side as her fear eased. She knew she could trust the support she would find when she allowed herself to be vulnerable.

☙ Closing Reflection — The Strength of Vulnerability: Building Trust through Openness

Vulnerability is not the absence of strength, it's the bridge that connects hearts and builds trust. Biscuit's trembling during the fireworks wasn't a display of fear, it was an act of faith. She trusted that I would stay, that she could lean into vulnerability and still be safe. That moment reminded me that trust and vulnerability are inseparable.

As leaders, and as people, we often strive to appear composed and capable. But when we allow others to see our uncertainty, we invite connection. The courage to admit "I need help" or "I don't know" doesn't diminish credibility, it deepens it. It shows that we value honesty over image and growth over perfection.

In times of crisis, like the aftermath of the I-35W bridge collapse, I learned that transparency and vulnerability lay the foundation for healing. When leaders are open about what they don't yet know or understand, but remain committed to learning, connection and trust can grow deeper.

Biscuit's fear and trembling during loud fireworks displays reminded me that vulnerability is not weakness, it is courage. It's the doorway to deeper connection, resilience, and servant leadership. In her willingness to lean on me, Biscuit taught me that the greatest strength of a leader is found in the simple, powerful act of being vulnerable.

The strongest leaders are not the ones without fear, they're the ones who stay close enough for others to lean on when they feel fear. Vulnerability will always open the door to trust, and trust opens the way to transformation. This is servant leadership.

🐾 Pawprint Practice — The Strength of Vulnerability

Pause and Reflect: In one appropriate setting, admit a limitation, a mistake, or a place where you need support. Allow others to meet you there without apology or explanation.

Lead with Openness: Identify one area in your life or leadership where you feel pressure to appear strong. What might happen if you let others see your vulnerability instead?

Practice Receiving: This week, let someone support you. It might be as simple as accepting help, sharing a struggle, or saying, "I don't have all the answers."

Build Trust through Transparency: Vulnerability is the birthplace of trust. When you share authentically, even a small truth about uncertainty, you invite others to do the same.

Model Biscuit's Courage: Just as Biscuit leaned into care instead of pulling away during her moments of fear, find moments to lean into the comfort and wisdom of others. You'll discover that vulnerability doesn't drain strength, it multiplies it.

Act with Grace: When others open up to you, respond with gentleness, not advice. Listening deeply is one of the purest ways to honor someone's courage to be vulnerable.

"True strength is not in how tightly we hold ourselves together, but in how bravely we allow ourselves to be held."

Chapter 6

The Joy of Play: Creating a Positive and Uplifting Environment

"A dog wags its tail with its heart."
— *Martin Buxham*

Biscuit loved to play. Whether it was chasing a tennis ball across the yard, racing up and down her hill, or rolling on her back with paws in the air, she approached every moment with unfiltered joy. Her tail wagged not just in excitement, but in invitation. She had this uncanny way of saying, *"Come on, lighten up a little. Life's not that serious."*

One of my favorite memories came after the first snowfall each year. The moment the door opened, Biscuit would dash into the yard, plunging her nose into the snow and tossing it skyward. Then, with a delighted snort, she'd roll onto her back, wriggling in the snow like she was making her own version of snow angels. We'd chase each other around her hill, laughing as snow flew in every direction. For those few minutes, everything else in the world fell away.

Her playfulness wasn't about distraction, it was about connection. She didn't care how long my day had been or how heavy the world felt. When she dropped her ball at my feet, she wasn't asking for entertainment, she was offering a joyful invitation to play. And every time I said yes, I remembered something vital: joy isn't separate from leadership, it's part of it.

One evening after an especially demanding week, I came home mentally drained. Reports, meetings, and decisions had consumed every ounce of focus. I walked in the door, and there she was, ball in mouth, tail sweeping the floor. I sighed, ready to collapse, but her eyes gleamed with hope. The moment I tossed that ball, something shifted. The weight began to lift. Ten minutes later, I was laughing for the first time all week. Biscuit reminded me that joy is a form of renewal.

Leaders sometimes forget the value of lightheartedness. We get caught up in goals, deadlines, and responsibilities. But people are drawn to those who radiate warmth and lightheartedness. Biscuit reminded me that bringing joy to a team, or a home, brings fuel to relationships. It keeps people engaged, connected, and willing to give their best.

Her sense of fun reminded me that a positive environment isn't optional, it's foundational. Playfulness doesn't diminish professionalism; it enhances connection. A culture where laughter and fun are welcome becomes a place where trust and creativity thrive. When people feel free to laugh, they also feel free to contribute, innovate, and belong.

Biscuit didn't have to try to lift spirits, she simply lived in the moment. Her joyfulness inspired everyone around her to be the same. She showed me that positivity, when practiced with sincerity, can transform a room, a team, or even an organization.

💬 Personal Reflection

Biscuit's playfulness was contagious. Her joy rippled outward, lightening hearts and softening even the most serious moments. Being with her inspired me to create spaces, at home and at work, where laughter and connection were part of the culture.

Humor, I discovered, isn't just entertainment, it's an antidote to pressure and a bridge to connection. Sharing a humorous moment or story with someone, or a group, signals an openness that can lead to other positive interactions. The openness they feel can make them feel seen, safe, and valued.

Anyone who knows me knows I'm a lifelong baseball fan, and I would be very excited on opening day of the baseball season because all teams were starting with the same record. I felt it was a great opportunity to interact directly with employees in a lighthearted way and inject joy into the workplace. At MnDOT, I'd invite the President of the Minnesota Twins to speak with employees about the upcoming season, and then my leadership team and I would make the rounds, peanuts and Cracker Jacks in hand, singing *"Take Me Out to the Ball Game"* as we went from floor to floor, tossing the goodies to people at their desks.

At first, employees weren't sure what to make of it. But by the next year, people were waiting for us, ready to join in our brigade. Some brought guitars or drums, and we had a huge troupe of people walking and singing together. A full parade of laughter and song echoed through the halls. That simple act of play became a symbol of connection and shared spirit. It also showed everybody that it is okay to laugh in their workspace.

Interestingly, the same scenario played out at the NDDOT when my leadership team and I went from desk to desk singing and giving out treats to celebrate the upcoming baseball season. The organization didn't matter, people responded the same way, enjoying the joyful connection with leadership and simply having fun.

The same kind of joy shows up in unexpected places. I first met Mary Mancuso on the pickleball court. My wife and I were newcomers to the sport, and Mary and her husband John welcomed us warmly. As we got to know Mary, I quickly realized that she was demonstrating the characteristics of a servant leader in our pickleball group. She was a natural servant leader: open, empathetic, and full of humor. She cared deeply about everyone she met. Before her retirement, Mary worked in the healthcare industry, taking care of others. Her openness, welcoming nature, and curiosity really drew people to her. Most importantly, she was spreading joy within the pickleball group.

Our group had two playing levels, beginner/intermediate and advanced, and Mary made sure to bridge both. She got to know people and how they felt by asking questions, without being intrusive. She always encouraged players, learned their stories, and noticed when someone needed a chance. When one intermediate player longed to move up, after he was told no many times, Mary quietly arranged it, bringing joy to his heart and harmony to the group. Her kindness turned a simple pastime into a community.

Mary reminded me that servant leaders appear in all walks of life. I never would have guessed that I would have met one of the best servant leaders ever on the pickleball court.

Play also showed up in the workplace in unexpected, funny ways. Being able to laugh at yourself can also create a great environment for servant leadership. Once, I decided to create a "Hall of Servant Leadership" in the main office building of MnDOT. There was a particular hallway that housed most of the leadership team, and I wanted it to be a space to showcase our values through art, quotes, and symbols. I scheduled an open house for employees to walk through the hallway, but felt one thing was missing: some inviting red velvet curtains to frame the hallway like an old movie theater entrance.

I climbed the ladder to hang them myself, only to have the entire setup come crashing down. When I turned around, my leadership team was doubled over laughing.

I climbed down, sat on the floor, and joined them. Soon, the hallway was full of laughter, deep, uncontrollable, joyful laughter. What started out as frustration became one of the most memorable moments of my career. Laughter connects us because it reminds us we're all human.

Biscuit's joy taught me that play restores perspective. It clears space for creativity, trust, and renewal. When we laugh, we loosen our grip on control, and that's where true connection grows.

 Closing Reflection — Joy as the Bridge to Trust

Joy is more than laughter, it is leadership in motion. Biscuit showed me that playfulness opens hearts faster than any meeting agenda ever could. When leaders make space for joy, they build cultures where trust and belonging thrive.

Her joy was simple yet powerful. She reminded me that the best leaders aren't those who carry the most weight, but those who know how to lighten it, for themselves and for others. A wagging tail, a shared laugh, or a spontaneous song can shift an entire room, and sometimes that's all it takes to lead with joy.

In leadership, joy is both permission and promise. It gives people permission to bring their full selves to work and promises them that connection matters as much as performance. When leaders share laughter, they send a message of connection: *You belong here. You are valued.*

Like Biscuit during a snowfall, rolling around, running up and down her hill, reveling in the moment, we can choose to lead with delight. Because when we lead with joy, we invite others to shine. The best leaders don't silence joy, they amplify it, which turns ordinary moments into extraordinary trust and connection.

 Pawprint Practice — Leading with Lighthearted Purpose

Pause and Reflect: In a moment when frustration would be your default response, pause and offer warmth instead, through humor, kindness, or shared vulnerability. How did it shift your energy or the energy of others?

Bring Joy to Leadership: Intentionally spark joy this week. Celebrate small wins, share gratitude, or open a meeting with humor. Watch how connection deepens when joy is present.

Model Biscuit's Presence: Like Biscuit, don't force fun, invite it. Let your lightheartedness set the tone for warmth, safety, and belonging.

Heal Through Play: When tension rises, choose laughter over correction. Tell a story, share a moment of humility, or offer a lighthearted pause. Play disarms fear and fosters trust.

Reflect and Renew: At the end of each day, ask yourself: *Did I lift someone's spirit today? Did I create space for joy?* The answers will point to where your leadership shines most.

"Joy isn't the opposite of work, it's the heartbeat that keeps service alive."

Chapter 7

Facing Challenges Together: Strength in Teamwork

True teamwork is built in the trenches. It isn't just about collaboration when things go smoothly, it's about mutual support when the path is steep. Biscuit never left my side when storms came, literally or emotionally. And in that, she reminded me that servant leadership is rooted in solidarity.

Her example mirrored the heart of servant leadership: no one moves ahead until everyone can move together.

One winter afternoon, snow piled higher than expected. I was trying to shovel a path, exhausted and overwhelmed. Biscuit bounded out, nose covered in flakes, and began running through the drifts ahead of me, clearing just enough space for me to follow. She wasn't solving the problem, she was joining in, reminding me that real teamwork isn't about removing the challenge, but carrying it together. Step by step, we made our way through. More importantly, her presence lifted my spirit. What had started out as a chore became a shared adventure.

That simple scene became a living metaphor for teamwork. Leadership is about creating an environment where people feel safe to contribute, where everyone's effort matters, and where joy is part of the process. In my years of public service, especially through moments of crisis, I saw that same truth: when people felt valued and trusted, they brought their best selves forward. Teams built on fear fracture, teams built on trust flourish.

Biscuit never saw life as a solo journey. From her earliest days, she treated everyone she met, dogs, people, even the mail carrier, as part of her team. When the mail truck appeared each day, she ran to greet it, tail wagging. At first, our mail carrier wasn't sure what to think, but soon she began bringing a treat for Biscuit. It wasn't long before there was a smile on both faces, two teammates connected through kindness. Biscuit simply believed everyone belonged.

She was a natural collaborator. When another dog joined her on Biscuit Hill, she didn't compete for dominance, she adapted. She paused, studied, then synced. If the other dog barked, Biscuit joined in, not to escalate, but to reassure: *I'm with you.* That was her version of teamwork, not taking over, not backing away, but showing up with presence and purpose. And with that, calm followed.

Teamwork, at its core, is collaboration in action, the willingness to carry one another's burdens, celebrate each other's victories, and remain steady when things go wrong. It's understanding that leadership is less about being the best and more about bringing out the best in others. Biscuit lived that daily, quietly, faithfully, and joyfully. Whether greeting a guest, welcoming another dog into her space, or waiting patiently for a child to catch up, she made room for others. She modeled inclusive strength, not through command, but through connection.

Her teamwork was also protective. When our son was sick, Biscuit seemed to know. She moved between all of us, checking emotions, never demanding, always offering calm. She created a network of care simply by being a steady presence. Everyone felt part of something bigger because Biscuit made belonging easy and real.

Even at the end of her life, she showed the deepest form of teamwork, allowing others to care for her. She accepted help with quiet grace, teaching us that vulnerability is also part of the team experience. Mutual support, not independence, gives strength its staying power.

That's the kind of teamwork that changes organizations and lives alike, the kind that lifts rather than competes, that listens instead of lectures, that stays when it would be easier to walk away.

Every great team has a Biscuit, someone who listens, connects, and brings out the best in others simply by believing in them. She never tried to lead alone, she led *with* us. And that made all the difference.

Personal Reflection

The same truths I learned from Biscuit carried into my professional life. The best teams I've ever been part of weren't those that avoided hardship, they were the ones that faced it together.

At MnDOT as well as NDDOT, there were long days, heavy emotions, and moments of deep uncertainty. Yet people kept showing up for one another. There were no heroic speeches, just small, human acts of care: a cup of coffee left on a desk, a quiet *"You okay?"* in the hallway. Those moments mattered more than any policy or plan. They built safety, and from that safety came resilience.

After the I-35W bridge collapse, our agency faced unimaginable pressure. Fear and fatigue could have divided us, but something extraordinary happened instead. Engineers, planners, maintenance crews, and communications staff all came together. There were no silos, no egos, just shared purpose: to serve, to restore, and to rebuild. Every act of collaboration, a kind word, an extra hour, a willingness to listen, became the thread that held us together.

Three outstanding professionals that I had the honor to work with stand out as powerful servant leaders: Khani Sahebjam, Bernie Arseneau, and Ron Henke. All three served as my Deputies. As the leader of the DOT, I needed leaders in these roles who embodied servant leadership and who were respected by the employees. Each had different personalities and strengths, but all were lifelong public servants devoted to collaboration. When I first introduced the concept of servant leadership, they seemed curious, even skeptical. But soon they recognized those values within themselves and began to model them with focus and intention. They became ambassadors of servant leadership in action, elevating teamwork across our agencies and inspiring employees and stakeholders alike.

Khani, Bernie, and Ron all excelled at building relationships at our state legislatures, and they bridged the gaps between political parties. They were respected by our political leaders because of their knowledge of the agencies and their people. Legislators leaned on them as transportation experts. As the new political appointee, they also paved the way for me to be successful in my role. The relationships they built provided an amazing amount of legislative support for the DOTs, which was especially needed in Minnesota after the collapse. The trust they built led to strong support of our budget and programs, in turn leading to employees feeling good about where they worked. Their servant leadership was oftentimes quietly working in the background, but it was truly effective.

One of the highest-performing teams I ever worked with was the Transportation Planning Team for the Olympic Winter Games in Salt

Lake City. Representing federal transportation agencies, I was part of a massive coordination effort involving local, state, and national partners. There were layers of agencies involved due to the complexity of providing for safety, movement of athletes and visitors, creating the venue locations, and responding to dignitary requests. Working within the context of the Olympic Transportation Group, I learned to function as a true servant leader and realized that there was a time to lead, and a time to follow.

Political support for the games was at a very high level. In my role, I supported the President's Olympic Task Force. As part of the Olympic Transportation Team, we adopted the mantra, *"Failure is not an option,"* since the games were coming and there wasn't any room for delay. Every agency, every participant operated as equals, and that's what made this such a unique team effort. Yet despite the pressure, our collaboration was joyful. We had fun working in this dynamic environment. Servant leadership guided our efforts, and the results showed. The games ran smoothly, and years later, when I meet someone from that team, the first word we use is still *"we."*

Teamwork, too, defined some of my most meaningful personal experiences. While living in Albany, New York, I was invited to field a baseball team for the National Senior Men's World Series in Minnesota. I quickly recruited players, many former college or pro athletes who I felt would be great teammates and represent servant leadership on the ball field. As we headed to Minnesota, we had only practiced several times and had no real games under our belt, but we had enthusiasm as we headed toward the World Series.

We finished fourth among eight established teams, which was an amazing feat for a newly formed group. Looking back, it wasn't talent alone that carried us, it was shared purpose, humility, teamwork, and care for one another. And we all entered this adventure with the mindset that we wanted to enjoy the moment and have fond memories of the experience, which we did. Servant leadership was alive on that ball field.

I've seen the principle of teamwork come alive countless times. What made the difference wasn't structure or system, it was tone. It was the shared spirit of *we're in this together*. Like Biscuit, we learned that success happens when people feel trusted to contribute their part. True teamwork is never about hierarchy or titles, it's about shared purpose and goals.

When leaders choose to walk *with* their people instead of ahead of them, they build communities that endure.

 Closing Reflection — Standing Shoulder to Shoulder

There was never a day Biscuit didn't understand the strength of *we*. Whether running beside us, waiting her turn, or nudging another forward, she embodied what teamwork truly means: trust in motion.

True teamwork is built in the small, unseen moments: the shared effort, shared purpose, the unspoken encouragement, and the steady presence in all situations. It's not about being the loudest voice, but the one who listens, lifts, and leads with intention.

The strongest teams don't form from perfection, but from presence. Members choose to stay when things get hard, to listen when tensions rise, and to believe in one another even when outcomes are uncertain. Those are the teams that last, built not by competition, but by compassion and trust.

Biscuit embodied teamwork instinctively. She stayed close with focus and purpose, bringing joy to all she met.

May we all lead the way Biscuit lived, standing together, moving together, and finding strength not in being first, but in belonging as a team. Because in every challenge lies an opportunity to lead with purpose. When we walk together, no hill is too steep, and no storm too strong.

🐾 Pawprint Practice — Strength in Teamwork

Pause and Reflect: Identify one responsibility this week that you've been carrying alone and intentionally invite someone else into it. Practice naming what you need and trusting the strength of the team.

Build Connection: Look for small ways to strengthen bonds, listen deeply, share encouragement, and notice how inclusion transforms effort into unity.

Share Leadership: Like Biscuit running beside her companions rather than ahead, practice leading *with* others, not over them. Ask for input, invite collaboration, and recognize contributions openly.

Foster Mutual Trust: When tensions arise, respond with calm and compassion. Model steadiness, transparency, and gratitude, the traits that allow teams to thrive even in storms.

Celebrate Together: Mark small wins. Acknowledge each other's efforts. Remind everyone that the success of one belongs to all.

"Every small act of teamwork leaves an imprint. Each act says, *We're in this together.*"

Chapter 8

The Gift of Presence:
Leading by Example

"Dogs don't tell us how to live — they show us."
— *Unknown*

Biscuit never led with noise or command. She led through quiet, consistent example. Her calm was her compass, and her actions were her message. She didn't seek to be noticed, yet everyone noticed her. There was a steadiness about her that seemed to invite people, and even other dogs, to follow suit. If there was tension, she absorbed it. If there was uncertainty, she waited. She showed that leadership begins not with direction, but by demonstration.

One of the most striking ways Biscuit led by example was in her patience with adults. She seemed to sense when people were anxious or impatient, and instead of matching their energy, she modeled stillness. When friends came to the house and conversations grew lively or loud, Biscuit would simply lie down in the center of the room, her head resting on her paws, breathing deeply as if to say, *It's all right, slow down.* Gradually, voices softened. People leaned back in their chairs. Her presence shifted the room from haste to peace. She didn't correct anyone, she simply offered a better way to be.

She also taught the art of waiting. Whether for a walk, a meal, or when we stopped to talk with friends, Biscuit never pushed or complained. She would sit patiently, tail gently sweeping the floor, eyes fixed with quiet trust. Watching her made me realize how much of leadership is about waiting, trusting timing, allowing space for others to grow, and believing that what is meant to unfold will do so when the time is right. Her patience and presence weren't passive, they were powerful. They carried a quiet confidence that everything would work out as it should.

Another unforgettable moment came the day Biscuit found her way back to me at the dog park. The park was large and wooded, and she had wandered farther than usual chasing a scent. As the sun began to fade, I called for her again and again, my voice swallowed by the trees. Just as dusk settled, I saw her trotting calmly up the hill, mud on her paws, ears perked, tail wagging in easy rhythm. She didn't appear panicked or lost. She simply followed her own sure path home, confident and unhurried, as though she trusted she was not lost, knowing I would be waiting.

Her return wasn't luck, it was instinct, faith, and composure in action. She had led herself home, showing me that patience is best. Watching her that evening, I thought about how leadership often asks us to do the same: to stay composed when the path disappears, to trust our principles when the map is unclear, and to walk forward so that others might find courage in our steadiness. Some call this following your North Star. Biscuit didn't just find her way back, she reminded me that knowing who you are will always guide you to where you belong.

People rarely remember what is said in moments of pressure, but they always remember the behavior. During my years in public leadership, especially in times of crisis, I often reflected on how Biscuit would react: with calm, with patience, with presence. I tried to listen more than I spoke, to respond thoughtfully instead of reacting quickly, and to project steadiness when uncertainty loomed. Her silent leadership became my model for how to steady others, not through control, but through consistency.

Biscuit's life illustrated that example builds trust faster than words ever could. Her patience invited reflection. Her steadiness created peace. Her return home proved that confidence rooted in presence will always lead in the right direction. She lived each day with quiet authenticity, teaching everyone around her what true presence looks like. She didn't need authority to lead, she received authority because she was believable. Her actions aligned with her nature, and that consistency was her greatest influence.

Watching Biscuit live her values reminded me that leading by example isn't a theory to study, it's a daily choice: to embody the principles we hope others will see in us.

💭 Personal Reflection

Stephen M. R. Covey wrote about the four cores of credibility of trust: integrity, intent, capability, and results. Two of those, integrity and intent, are the foundation of leading by example.

Integrity is not only how we behave when everyone is watching, it's how we behave when no one is. And intent reveals whether we serve ourselves or others. People quickly discern the difference. Those who act from self-interest may lead in title, but never with moral authority. True servant leaders lead with integrity and intent that serve the greater good.

Mary Peters served as the United States Department of Transportation (USDOT) Secretary of Transportation. I first got to know Mary when she was the Federal Highway Administrator. Mary quickly became one of my mentors, and I learned the power of servant leadership simply by watching how she led. When I served as the agency's mega project team leader, I interacted with her frequently because these were considered high-risk projects at the federal level. Whenever I visited with her, she was always the most welcoming and thoughtful person, someone who exhibited kindness in everything she did. I always thought how unusual this was for someone who had achieved the pinnacle position in the transportation industry, but then I realized, that is exactly how she got there.

During the response, recovery, and rebuild of the I-35W bridge collapse, I continued to interact with Mary as the Secretary. She was no different during that time of crisis, always kind and respectful to everybody who was trying to do the best they could during a very challenging time. Her calmness was exactly what was needed at the federal level to provide support to the state and local officials. To walk in with a command-and-control "take over" mentality would have been disastrous.

Leading by example was one of Mary's strengths, and it was something I carried with me in my servant leadership journey, especially when I found myself leading two DOTs. She was a wonderful mentor to me.

When I led MnDOT and the NDDOT, I carried that same principle with me. I saw countless examples of people who lived servant leadership daily, often quietly, often unseen. To honor them, I created the *Heroes Program*, celebrating those who went above and beyond in service to others. We held the event at the Capitol, invited honorees' families, and asked the Governors to speak. It was a celebration of the honorees' humility and courage to do the right things at all times, and their successes as they led by example. During these ceremonies, there wasn't a dry eye in the room.

Every year, one group stood out: our snowplow operators, often called *snow fighters*. These were the people who ensured the public could travel safely during the fiercest of storms. Each snowplow operator had a story of something remarkable they did to save lives. As they cleared the roads, they always ran into unique situations that required them to respond as servant leaders, including making sure emergency responders could do their jobs accessing people in need. They braved blizzards, worked holidays, and risked their own safety to keep roads clear so others could travel safely. They didn't ask for recognition. They simply showed up, again and again, when their communities needed them most. Their dedication was a living example of servant leadership: faithful, humble, and strong.

When asked what kept me up at night as a DOT leader, my answer was always the same: *a major storm that could endanger lives.* Knowing our snowplow operators were out there gave me peace. They were servant leaders in orange jackets, leading by quiet example, never for attention, always for love of service. Like Biscuit, they didn't lead for recognition; they led because it was the right thing to do for the communities they served.

Leading by example was the hallmark of Biscuit's life too, subtle but powerful. If we live each day with integrity and positive intent, we too will earn the moral authority that defines a true servant leader.

◠ Closing Reflection — The Light of Example

Biscuit's life was a master class in unspoken leadership. Because of Biscuit's ability to earn respect, she changed the atmosphere wherever she went. Her patience steadied impatience; her confidence quieted fear. She showed that true leaders don't seek to impress, they inspire through who they are, moment by moment.

Leadership is rarely about what we say, it's about what we do and how people feel in our presence. Whenever Biscuit entered a room, people felt peace. When she walked beside me on the trail, I felt steadier. She didn't change circumstances, but she transformed how we moved through them. Her example proved that influence isn't measured by how loudly we speak, but by how faithfully we live our values when no one is watching.

Leading by example means living with integrity quietly, the way Biscuit carried trust without performance or pretense. It's being dependable in uncertainty, being kind when it's not required, and steady when others falter. Leadership, at its best, becomes a mirror reflecting the best in others.

When I picture Biscuit trotting calmly up that hill in the fading light, I see the perfect image of leadership through presence. She didn't need direction because she trusted her compass. She knew the way because she had walked it before, with faith, consistency, and purpose.

True leaders, like Biscuit, remind us that presence is power. When we live our values with quiet confidence, we give others permission to do the same. We steady our families, our teams, and our communities through trust earned by example.

May we all lead the way Biscuit lived, faithful in spirit, calm in action, and unwavering in integrity. A steady life, lived with purpose and integrity, can light the way home for many. The truest form of leadership is presence, silent and steady.

🐾 Pawprint Practice — Leading by Example

Pause and Reflect: In one stressful moment this week, slow your pace, steady your tone, and respond with intention. Let others take their clues from your calm.

Model Patience: When progress feels stalled or tension rises, resist the urge to rush ahead. Wait and embrace stillness, trusting that good outcomes unfold in their time.

Trust the Path: When uncertainty clouds direction, return to your core values. Let integrity, not impulse, guide your steps.

Lead with Consistency: Show up the same way each day: honest, kind, and reliable. Consistency builds credibility faster than words ever can.

Inspire through Action: Let your behavior teach. A simple act of grace, empathy, or courage can inspire more deeply than any command.

"Every quiet act of integrity and leading by example becomes a lesson someone else will remember."

Chapter 9

Courage and Sacrifice:
The Heart of Service

"Some heroes wear capes. Mine wore fur."
— Unknown

Courage doesn't always announce itself. Sometimes it arrives quietly, disguised as devotion. Biscuit's courage was like that: steady, instinctive, and rooted in trust. She didn't need to be fearless to be brave. Her courage was born from loyalty, from the simple conviction that she had a role to play in the lives of people she cared about. She showed it in small, consistent ways that revealed a deeper truth: that real courage often comes from the heart of sacrifice and service.

I'll never forget the times she stepped between me and other dogs when she sensed tension or threat. It was never aggression, it was protection. Her body would stiffen slightly, her eyes lock in quiet watchfulness. She would position herself close enough to say, *"I've got this."* I never doubted that she would defend me if needed. It wasn't about dominance or fear, it was about courage.

That same courage showed up again at the end of her life. Even when her body grew weak, her spirit stayed strong. Her legs trembled, and sometimes she stumbled, but when I entered the room, her tail still thumped, and she would try to rise, determined to greet me as she always had. Her eyes spoke a language of resilience, a heart unwilling to surrender its purpose. She didn't want sympathy, she wanted connection. That was her courage: the choice to keep showing up, even when it hurt.

Her strength had been tested early in life. As a puppy, Biscuit needed surgery on both knees. She was born without kneecaps, which made it difficult for her to bend her back legs. Her recovery was long, and her balance never perfect, yet she never slowed down. Wobbly knees and all, she ran with joy, played with abandon, and embraced life without hesitation. She embodied the kind of courage that doesn't deny difficulty, but simply refuses to be defined by it.

Years later, when she was diagnosed with immune-mediated hemolytic anemia, she nearly died. The day of her emergency transfusion is etched in my memory: the hum of machines, the stillness of the room, and her quiet eyes meeting mine as blood flowed into her veins. The odds were against her, but she survived. When she came home, she was weak, but wagging her tail, she looked up at me with gentle resolve, as if to say, *"I'm not done yet."* That moment taught me more about resilience than any leadership seminar ever could. Biscuit didn't fight for life out of fear of losing it; she fought with courage, anchored in her purpose of service.

Her courage wasn't about conquering challenges. It was about enduring them with grace. She met every setback with patience, every obstacle with perseverance, and every pain with courage. Watching her, I realized that courage and sacrifice are inseparable. To serve others, to love deeply, is always a risk of losing something. It means giving without assurance, showing up when it's hard, and staying faithful even when strength fades. Biscuit lived that truth every day.

💭 Personal Reflection

True servant leadership is built on courage, not the kind that shouts, but the kind that sustains. It's the courage to care when others withdraw, to keep serving and sacrificing when weary, to take responsibility even when it would be easier to step aside. I've seen that same quiet strength in people who never sought the title of leader, but lived leadership daily through compassion and consistency.

Colonel Mark Nelson, Superintendent of the North Dakota Highway Patrol, embodied that kind of courage. Mark grew up in the organization, and his leadership style was recognized by the highest levels of state government when he was appointed to the Governor's cabinet as the Superintendent. Like many people in the Patrol, Mark had difficult encounters with the people he was trying to serve. In one such encounter, he almost lost his life. Despite this, Mark came back to demonstrate the ultimate sacrifice and courage to continue on. As he did, his heart became his guide even more, and his leadership softened into wisdom.

I later worked with Mark after his retirement from the Patrol, when he joined the North Dakota Department of Transportation as Deputy Director, overseeing non-engineering functions. As I got to know Mark, I quickly realized that he had a huge heart that translated into deep respect from all the employees. Just as he had done with the State Patrol, he was firm when needed, but he showed kindness and empathy in doing so. Because he led from his heart, he was always open to new ideas and suggestions, including anything that could make him a better leader.

Mark was always recognized as a champion for all the units he supervised, and he made sure their presence was felt throughout the DOT. After an assessment of our leadership team, one person was consistently mentioned by employees for his servant leadership: Mark Nelson.

Just like me, Mark was also a staunch advocate for traffic safety. He devoted his entire life to helping others and saving lives. When I arrived at NDDOT, there was an outstanding traffic safety staff under Mark's leadership. We had many discussions about how to elevate our approach to reducing fatalities. Our Director of Highway Safety, Karin Mongeon, had always wanted to start a "Vision Zero" approach to our programs and projects, with strategies to reduce fatalities. All three of us worked hand in hand to provide leadership for this effort. Mark was the recognized champion for traffic safety, and because of his servant leadership approach, the initiative was launched and just took off. Very quickly, a new safety culture had been embedded into the agency and the number of crashes was reduced, thanks to Mark's leadership.

Courage and sacrifice also defined one of the hardest seasons of my public service, the 2011 Minnesota state government shutdown. For twenty days, nearly 22,000 state employees were furloughed. Only essential services remained. As MnDOT Commissioner, I worked with my leadership team to retain just enough staff to handle emergencies, but nearly every project halted. Morale plummeted.

Frustration spread. Those furloughed were angry at the politics, and those who stayed felt burdened by the strain of managing all essential duties to keep our roads and bridges safe. During a visit to our Twin Cities District Office, I met with maintenance crews who were discouraged and considering slowing their work in protest. After discussing the broader impact on public safety, they made a remarkable choice to continue serving the public with full dedication. Their courage and selflessness mirrored Biscuit's quiet resolve: *do the right thing, even when it is difficult.*

When the shutdown ended, healing became our new task. Across the state, we greeted returning employees at their entrances. I stood beside Deb Ledvina, whose kindness had anchored many through that time. As each person walked through the door, I shook their hand and thanked them for coming back. Emotion welled up, and tears fell, not from exhaustion, but gratitude. Despite hardship, our people had remained true to their calling to serve the State of Minnesota. MnDOT's heart still beat strong.

Reflecting on those years, I've learned that the most courageous acts often go unseen. They're in the ones who stay late to ensure others are safe, who tell the truth when it's hard, who choose what's right over what's easy. That's the courage of conviction, the willingness to sacrifice comfort for integrity.

Through every crisis, I often thought of Biscuit's steadiness. She didn't posture or panic. She simply stood where she was needed. Her quiet strength guided me through many storms. Leadership isn't about fearlessness, it's about faithfulness. It's showing up even when you're uncertain, because others are counting on you.

Like Biscuit, courageous leaders lead with heart. They don't measure sacrifice by what they lose, but by what they give.

 ## Closing Reflection — The Heart of Service

Courage and sacrifice live at the center of servant leadership. Biscuit never announced her bravery, she simply lived it. She protected, endured, and gave, again and again, without expectation of return. Her body weakened, but her spirit never did. She showed that service, when rooted in love, outlasts pain, fear, and even time itself.

To serve others is to have the courage to embrace vulnerability, to risk disappointment, fatigue, and heartbreak for the sake of something greater. Biscuit taught me that this kind of courage doesn't drain us, it defines us. It fills life with meaning because it connects us to others through compassion and faithfulness.

The heart of service isn't perfection, it's devotion. It's showing up one more time, loving one more time, giving one more time, even when it hurts. Biscuit's courage was always about devotion.

Courage isn't about being unafraid, it's about loving something enough to keep going anyway. May we all find that same courage within ourselves, the courage to serve humbly, to give without keeping score, and to keep faith when the road grows steep. Because service given that endures through sacrifice is the purest form of servant leadership there is.

Pawprint Practice — Courage and Sacrifice

Pause and Reflect: Say yes to one act of service this week that stretches your comfort zone, but aligns with your values. Step into it with clarity, compassion, and courage.

Serve Beyond Comfort: Find one opportunity to help someone or speak truth when silence would be easier. Courage begins with a single step.

Honor Your Strength: In a situation where you feel weary or discouraged, choose to stay present and continue with integrity, instead of withdrawing.

Lead Through Presence: When others feel anxious or afraid, be the calm center. Sometimes leadership simply means standing when it would be easier to sit.

Sacrifice for Love: Give your time, patience, or heart to strengthen someone else's journey. True service always costs something, but it's a price worth paying.

"Every quiet act of courage strengthens the heartbeat of service in the world."

Chapter 10

Empathy in Action: Seeing the Heart

"A dog will teach you unconditional love. If you can have that in your
life, things won't be too bad."
— *Robert Wagner*

Empathy is the quiet bridge between hearts. It doesn't need
words, it simply needs patience and presence. Biscuit had that
gift. She seemed to feel what others felt and sensed emotions
before they were expressed. Her eyes told you she understood. Her soft
sighs, gentle nudges, and perfectly timed approaches carried an awareness
that went beyond instinct. She didn't analyze emotions, she absorbed
them, transformed them, and offered them back as comfort.

When my son was young and fell sick with the flu, Biscuit never left his
side. She curled against him, matching each slower breath with her own,
sometimes resting her head on his chest as if watching over every rise
and fall. She refused to go outside unless he stirred, as though her well-
being was tied to his. When he finally felt better, she greeted him with
quiet joy, a gentle tail wag and a soft lick to his hand, as if to say, *I knew
you'd be okay.* Her faithful presence was clearly empathy in action.

Later, when he struggled on the hockey rink, Biscuit sensed his frustration. After games that hadn't gone his way, she was always first at the door, tail wagging, eyes full of acceptance. She didn't judge or demand, she simply welcomed him home, and it didn't take long before Biscuit and Matt were running after balls in the yard. In those moments, she showed him that worth is never defined by performance, and that comfort sometimes comes best in silence.

Biscuit carried this same quiet empathy into her community with other dogs. On Biscuit Hill, where she often played and served as a gentle leader, her presence set the tone. When new dogs arrived, some nervous or unsure, she didn't rush in or dominate. She paused, studied, and approached slowly, inviting calm rather than competition. Her quietness settled the group, her confidence created harmony. Within minutes, tensions dissolved. What could have been chaos became peace. That was her way: leading through understanding, not authority or possessiveness of her hill.

Empathy is more than sensitivity, it's strength that listens. Biscuit's empathy wasn't fragile, it was powerful enough to transform the energy around her. When I came home after draining days at work, she greeted me with her familiar mix of playfulness and delight. Even if she had been begging for a walk earlier, she seemed to know when to shift gears, tail wagging, leash in mouth, eyes bright with determination. The moment we stepped outside, my fatigue lifted. Her joy was contagious. The heaviness of the day faded in the rhythm of our steps. It wasn't the walk that restored me, it was her presence. She always knew what I needed before I did.

Empathy, at its truest, is service. It notices without being asked, gives without condition, and heals through presence. Biscuit didn't try to fix emotions, she honored them. Whether offering stillness to a sick child, joy to a discouraged athlete, peace to unsure dogs, or companionship to a weary leader, she showed that empathy is not about feeling sorry, it is about feeling *with*.

Her quiet compassion held a message that transcends words: to serve others, we must first see their hearts.

As I reflect on Biscuit's quiet empathy, I'm reminded of moments in my own leadership journey when understanding another's heart changed everything. Watching her comfort my son when he was sick or greet him after a tough game showed me that true empathy doesn't require words, it simply requires presence. In my own life, I've learned how being fully present with others creates a space for healing, connection, and trust. Whether leading a team through uncertainty or supporting someone facing hardship, empathy often speaks louder than instruction. It bridges gaps, softens hearts, and reminds us that we are never alone.

During the Olympics in Salt Lake City, I served as a volunteer ombudsman with the Area Agency on Aging. I mediated issues between staff and residents in nursing homes and provided training to fellow volunteers on conflict management. Many interactions with the residents centered around food or cleanliness, basic needs that affected dignity and daily life. Though conflict never intimidated me, this environment was far from my comfort zone. I soon realized that trust built through empathy could make the biggest difference. When I listened fully, standing in both the resident's and staff's shoes, solutions emerged that felt fair and compassionate. It was challenging work, but also deeply rewarding. Empathy became the foundation of every resolution, and it transformed the experience for all involved.

Two remarkable servant leaders, Katherine Freund and Esther Greenhouse, have devoted their lives to helping older adults maintain independence through mobility, transportation, and enabling home environments.

I first met Katherine when I was a young engineer in Maine and helped her support a state legislative task force to address a wide range of transportation issues for the aging population. She later founded the Independent Transportation Network of America (ITN) to help bridge the mobility gap for people with transportation challenges. ITN focuses on community-based transportation solutions to bring people together, and has sustained itself for over 30 years.

I first connected with Esther through social media and, through the years, always tried to find opportunities to utilize her knowledge in the aging population space from a mobility perspective. An environmental gerontologist, she advocates designing living spaces, policies, and services that allow people to remain at home safely and confidently, because the status quo unnecessarily contributes to age-related decline and caregiving needs. She also leads Silver to Gold Strategies, which helps organizations better understand how aging shapes their business and their communities, ultimately supporting the aging population. Her strong academic background is matched by her practical approaches to serving others.

Though their backgrounds differ, Katherine and Esther share a defining trait: remarkable empathy. Their professional success is real and impressive, but it is their empathy that fuels it. They both have experiences in their past that required resilience and motivated them to become national leaders. They understand the lived experience that older adults face: the fears, hopes, and vulnerabilities, and they respond with creativity, dignity, and respect. Using their business savvy, they develop solutions that are truly life-changing. Individuals and organizations who work with them see their empathy, and that makes everyone better. These two remarkable women exhibit all the characteristics of servant leadership, and it is what is in their hearts that makes them so special.

Like Biscuit, I've come to understand that empathy is not a skill to master, but a way of seeing, a commitment to notice, to care, and to serve with heart. Her example reminds me daily that leadership grounded in empathy has the power to restore hope and strengthen the human spirit. The more I live and lead with empathy, the more I realize that Biscuit's greatest gift wasn't just comfort, it was the reminder that empathy itself is the deepest form of understanding.

Closing Reflection — The Gentle Power of Understanding

Empathy is the soul of servant leadership. It allows us to feel another's heart and respond with kindness instead of judgment. Biscuit lived that daily. She saw struggle and offered presence. She saw discouragement and met it with joy. Her empathy healed quietly because it was sincere.

The power of empathy lies in its quietness and connection. When we look beyond behavior to the emotion beneath, compassion takes root. That is where trust is built, healing begins, and community is strengthened.

Biscuit showed that empathy needs no words, only willingness to feel for others. In the gentle lean against my son, in her calming presence with nervous dogs, in her companionship after long days, she showed what empathy looks like when it listens.

To lead with empathy is to walk through life with open eyes and an open heart, to notice, understand, and to serve. Biscuit lived that calling, one gentle moment at a time. May we all learn to see with the heart, to sense what others need, to offer what comfort we can, and to meet the world with compassion that speaks louder than words. Those who see with the heart never walk alone.

Pause and Reflect: When someone feels withdrawn or unsettled this week, check in gently without pressing for answers. Let care open the door, not questions.

Listen Beyond Words: Notice emotion in tone, posture, and quiet energy as you interact with people on a daily basis.

Be Fully Present: When others share their struggles, resist the urge to solve. Simply be with them.

Reflect Peace: Like Biscuit on the hill, allow your calmness to shape the space you enter.

Give Joy Freely: A small encouragement, a smile, or a kind word can lift someone up more than you know.

"Empathy is love translated into understanding."

Chapter 11

Legacy of Love: The Lessons Biscuit Left

"Dogs come into our lives to teach us about love… they depart to teach us about loss. A new dog never replaces an old dog; it merely expands the heart."

— *Erica Jong*

Time has a way of softening the edges of grief. What once feels like unbearable loss slowly becomes gratitude, and what felt final becomes hope because of the memories we hold. After Biscuit passed, the house felt impossibly quiet, as though the heartbeat of our home had slipped away. Her toys sat untouched, her collar now empty, and her familiar routines dissolved overnight.

Love leaves traces. In every space she once occupied, there lingered a feeling, a warmth that reminded me she had been more than a companion. She had been a teacher, a mirror, a reminder of what it means to serve selflessly. Her presence changed not only how I led, but how I lived.

In the months after she was gone, I began to notice her influence everywhere. In moments of frustration, I'd think of her patience. In times of uncertainty, I'd recall her calm. And in times of sadness, I'd feel her gentle reassurance, all reminding me that service and love are never wasted. They live on in those who have been touched by others who embodied these gifts.

Biscuit's greatest lesson was love and how it influenced others. She didn't seek to be followed, but people, and even other animals, were naturally drawn to her. Her love built trust, healed tension, and invited peace wherever she went. She showed that the truest measure of a servant leader is not the projects completed or goals achieved, but the lives strengthened by their presence.

One evening, months after she was gone, I was cleaning out a drawer and found her old collar. The worn leather still carried her scent. I held it in my hands for a long time, feeling both the ache of missing her and the deep gratitude for having shared life with her. Her water dish, with "Biscuit" lettered on the side, sat nearby. That moment reminded me that leadership, too, is about letting go and trusting that what you've given will endure beyond you.

Throughout my public service journey, I often reflected on how love shapes legacy. The best leaders don't just build systems, they build people. They create cultures rooted in respect, kindness, and belonging. They remind others that service, at its heart, is an act of love. When leaders serve with genuine care, their influence ripples through generations. Just as Biscuit's presence continues to guide me, the example of loving leadership lives on in every person we've encouraged along the way.

Biscuit's legacy wasn't grand or loud, it was steady, faithful, and real. She left behind no possessions, no written words, no titles. What she left was far more powerful: the memory of her gentle eyes, the peace of her companionship, and the example of love expressed through action. That is the kind of legacy I hope to leave.

Love, when lived through service, outlasts time. It continues in the stories told, the kindnesses repeated, and the courage inspired in others. Biscuit's life was a reminder that leadership, in its highest form, is not about recognition, it's about loving relationships. She taught me that our most meaningful legacy is not what we leave *for* people, but what we leave *in* them.

💬 Personal Reflection

When I consider the lessons Biscuit left behind, I'm struck by how deeply her presence shaped who we became as a family and who I became as a leader.

Her legacy is not about singular accomplishments or dramatic moments. It is about the steady, quiet way she taught us how to love, how to trust, and how to keep showing up for one another. When she came into our lives, we had no idea how much she would reshape us. Yet day after day, year after year, she showed us what it meant to love and to lead through gentleness, loyalty, and heart.

I often think about how she influenced each member of our family in her own unique way. She offered comfort when we were hurting, companionship when we were lonely, and joy when we were ready to play. When my son struggled, she was there: silent, patient, but fully present. When life felt heavy for me, she nudged me outside, reminding me to breathe, to walk, and to find peace in simple moments. She never lectured. She never insisted. She simply lived love, and by doing so, invited us to live it too.

What continues to move me is how her legacy did not end when she passed. In the rawness of grief, we felt the depth of what she had given us. We were heartbroken, but beneath that sorrow was profound gratitude. We came to understand that her life was a gift, and like all true gifts, it left something behind: wisdom, courage, tenderness, and a desire to serve others the way she served us.

Even now, years later, I still ask myself what Biscuit would do. When faced with a difficult situation or a person in distress, I think about how Biscuit led: not with force, but with empathy, not with authority, but with presence. I can almost feel her at my side, steady and sure, reminding me to look beyond the surface, into the heart of things. Her example continues to guide my thoughts and decisions, especially when I'm faced with ambiguity or conflict.

Her legacy has followed us as we've moved from place to place. In each new town, as we meet new friends and neighbors, I notice her spirit slowly weaving into our interactions. It shows up in the way we welcome others, the way we listen, and the way we offer help before being asked.

Biscuit infused our family with a quiet expectation: to live generously, tenderly, and with courage.

I think about how her life overlapped my own seasons of growth. I was younger when Biscuit came into our home, full of ambition, eager to make my mark. Over time, as I moved into a new season of life, she reminded me that leadership isn't measured in titles or accomplishments, but in the effect we have on the people we touch. Her presence softened me, grounded me, and helped me see that true leadership begins at home, with those entrusted to us.

Now, as I enter my own senior years, I feel her legacy perhaps more deeply than ever. The pace of life has slowed, priorities have shifted, and still, her quiet wisdom speaks. She reminds me that I do not have to prove myself, I simply have to love, serve, and remain faithful to the people and places I'm given. That is enough.

Her legacy is not just a memory, it is a compass. It points toward compassion, humility, and connection. It reminds me that servant leadership isn't situational or temporary, it's a lifelong calling. Biscuit lived that truth from puppyhood through her final days, showing us that every moment is an opportunity to lead with love.

Her legacy continues to guide me, reminding me that a life of service is built not on big gestures, but on a thousand small ones offered with love.

 Closing Reflection — What Remains

Titles fade, projects end, and accomplishments are eventually forgotten, but love remains, love endures. Biscuit's love still lives in the lessons she taught, the calm she modeled, and the joy she brought into ordinary moments. Her life was a sermon without words, a daily reminder that love, when lived authentically, becomes the most powerful force of leadership.

The legacy of a servant leader is not measured by how long they lead, but by how deeply they loved. Biscuit's memory continues to guide me toward that truth. She showed that a legacy built on love doesn't need to be preserved, it continues naturally, in every life touched by it.

When I think of her now, I no longer feel sad. I feel gratitude. She came into my life for a reason, to teach me that leadership begins and ends with love. And though her paws no longer walk beside me, her presence remains in every act of compassion, every patient choice, and every moment of courage I can trace back to her example.

Her legacy lives in the hearts she touched, including mine.

And that, truly, is the mark of a life well lived.

🐾 Pawprint Practice — Legacy of Love

Reflect on Your Legacy: What lasting impression do you hope to leave on those you lead, love, and serve? Write down three words you'd want others to associate with your leadership.

Give Without Keeping Score: Choose one way this week to give quietly without recognition or reward. Let love, not obligation, guide your action.

Honor the Teachers: Reflect on those who have shaped your values. What lessons did they leave you? Consider sharing those lessons forward.

Lead with Heart: Before each decision, ask yourself: Does this choice build others up? Love leads through compassion, not control.

Live the Lesson: Like Biscuit, strive to make your presence a gift: calm in chaos, warmth in distance, light in darkness. That is how legacies are born.

"Every act of kindness, every moment of understanding, becomes part of your legacy of love. Lead so that others feel the heart behind your service."

Chapter 12

Becoming a Servant Leader: Applying Biscuit's Lessons

"The gift of a dog is not in teaching us how to live,
but in reminding us how to love."
— *Unknown*

Biscuit taught us that servant leadership is more than an inspiration, it is a daily practice. It begins with simple choices and small acts that shape how we show up for the people around us. In that spirit, this chapter offers a path forward, an invitation to apply what Biscuit lived so faithfully.

Becoming a servant leader doesn't happen overnight. It's a journey, a slow unfolding of the heart. It starts with small acts: listening before speaking, serving before expecting, giving before receiving. Over time, those choices become habits, and the habits become character. That's what Biscuit showed me. Her leadership wasn't found in any single act of bravery or obedience, it was revealed in her constancy, in the quiet way she lived and loved, day after day.

When I think about how to apply her lessons, I see how they align with the Seven Pillars of Servant Leadership I've tried to live and teach throughout my career. Each pillar: character, people-first mindset, skilled communication, compassion, foresight, systems thinking, and moral authority was reflected in her life in its simplest, most honest form. She had no need for titles or theory, she simply embodied what servant leadership looks like when it's rooted in love.

- She led through character, always steady and true to who she was.
- She placed people first, or in her case, every person she met, offering kindness without judgment.
- She practiced skilled communication through presence and attentiveness, teaching that listening is the most powerful form of connection.
- She modeled compassion, meeting everyone where they were.
- Her foresight came from awareness, sensing what others needed before they asked.
- She understood systems thinking instinctively, finding her place in the family "team" and maintaining harmony.
- And through all of it, she demonstrated moral authority, living by example rather than command.

Biscuit lived the pillars not through words, but through being. And isn't that what true leadership requires? Not perfection, but authenticity. Not dominance, but devotion. She showed me that leadership is not a position we earn, it's a responsibility we accept: to love, to guide, to serve.

Throughout my years in public service, I've seen leaders who embodied this calling and others who struggled to grasp it. The difference was always the same: those who led from love, built trust that lasted. Their initiatives were transformational and became embedded in the organization. Those who led from ego-built fear. Their initiatives were transactional and did not last. Love endures, fear dissolves. Servant leadership, at its heart, is love in motion, love that listens, supports, forgives, and uplifts.

As I reflect on Biscuit's life, I realize she taught me that every act of service, no matter how small, has the power to transform. Holding a door for someone, offering a kind word, pausing to truly listen, these are acts of leadership as surely as the grandest policy or program. When done with sincerity, they carry the same sacred weight. Biscuit didn't change the world, but she changed *my* world. And in doing so, she reminded me that the ripple of one small kindness can spread further than we can ever see.

We become servant leaders not by mastering others, but by mastering ourselves. It's about choosing humility when pride tempts us, patience when frustration rises, and forgiveness when judgment feels easier. It's about seeing every encounter as an opportunity to live out our values, to make love visible.

Every morning, as I begin my day, I think of Biscuit. I try to carry a bit of her spirit into the world, to listen more deeply, to walk more gently, to serve more fully. Because that's where leadership truly lives, not in speeches or titles, but in the quiet courage to live with love.

As I think about how Biscuit's teachings have shaped my life, I realize that becoming a servant leader is less about reaching a destination and more about choosing a way of being every day. It truly is a journey that never ends.

There is no diploma that certifies someone as a servant leader. No moment in time announces, *you've arrived.* Instead, servant leadership unfolds slowly, through small, intentional choices made again and again. Biscuit taught me that. She never set out to demonstrate a philosophy, she simply lived from the heart. And in doing so, she showed me that leadership grounded in service is not defined by what we accomplish, but by how we care for the people around us.

Looking at my life, year after year since her passing, the lessons continue to shape my actions. I recognize that leading with love, humility, and presence throughout my professional career was the very foundation of trust, collaboration, and real progress. When I listened deeply and served quietly, teams grew stronger. People felt seen. Solutions came more naturally. The work became more meaningful.

Over the years, I found that the most powerful way to lead was often through presence, being fully attentive to the needs and voices of others. It wasn't always easy. There were times I felt pressure to act quickly, to dictate rather than encourage. But Biscuit's example reminded me that the most lasting change comes when we slow down, pay attention, and respond with empathy. Her way of leading offered me a compass to move toward connection, not control. Serve first, and the path will reveal itself.

I've also come to understand that becoming a servant leader requires courage, the courage to put others before ourselves, and to remain patient in an impatient world. Biscuit demonstrated that courage as she faced her own challenges. From her early surgeries to her final days, she continued to give what she could. Even when her steps were slow and she grew unsteady, she still made her way to the door to greet me. That spirit taught me that leadership isn't about strength or perfection, it's about showing up with heart, no matter the circumstance.

Her lessons have followed me into new communities. Each time I've moved to a different city, I carried her spirit with me. I tried to meet people where they were, to listen before speaking, to look for ways, large or small, to be of service. I've found that when we lead with kindness and curiosity, doors open, relationships deepen, and lives intersect in ways that feel purposeful. In many ways, Biscuit still introduces me to people, guiding me to connect and serve wherever I am.

Applying her lessons has also changed how I view legacy. I once thought legacy was about achievement, about what we build or leave behind. Now I see it differently. Biscuit's legacy was not made of things, it was made of love. She left no material possessions, no accolades, no grand accomplishments. What she left was better: a lasting example of how to live with humility, empathy, and joy. That is a legacy that endures.

The longer I live, the more clearly I see that becoming a servant leader is not a task to complete, it is a daily practice. Some days we do it well, other days we fall short. But every day offers another opportunity to try again, to choose kindness, to listen deeply, to serve with a willing heart. Biscuit showed me that the most powerful leadership is not found on stages or in boardrooms, it is found in the quiet spaces where one life gently supports another.

Her example continues to steady my steps, reminding me that I can honor her life each time I choose compassion, presence, and service to others.

These lessons continue to guide me, and now they belong to you as well. The invitation is simple: carry them into your own life, and let love lead the way.

◌ Closing Reflection — The Journey Continues

Every story has an ending, but leadership never really ends. It continues through the lives we've touched, the kindnesses we've given, and the lessons we've shared. Biscuit's story is no different. Though her paws no longer leave prints in the snow, her spirit continues to guide the way, one act of compassion, one moment of courage, one quiet gesture of love at a time.

Becoming a servant leader means embracing that journey. It's not about achieving perfection, but about practicing presence: being aware, available, and authentic. It's choosing to see the good, nurture it, and pass it on.

Biscuit's lessons were never complicated. They were simple and intuitive, focused on kindness, patience, faithfulness, and serving with love. She taught us to be ready for the moment, and when it comes, to lead by example.

That is how a servant leader is made, not in the boardroom or on the stage, but in the small, sacred moments of everyday life.

Becoming a servant leader is a journey that begins new each day. When you offer presence, compassion, and courage, you carry forward the same spirit Biscuit shared so freely. These choices, small but faithful, create ripples of hope that reach far beyond what we can see.

The story now continues with you, in the way you listen, love, and serve those around you. May her story continue to inspire all who read it, to see with the heart, lead with love, and walk gently through the world, leaving pawprints of grace wherever they go.

🐾 Pawprint Practice — Becoming a Servant Leader

Start with Awareness: Notice where you have influence, at home, at work, or in your community. Leadership begins wherever compassion is needed.

Lead by Example: Choose one servant leadership characteristic that reflects your best self and practice it daily by showing up. Let your consistency become your credibility.

Listen with Love: In your next conversation, listen without planning your reply. Let understanding come before response.

Serve First: Ask, "How can I help?" before "What do I need?" Service rooted in humility builds connection and trust.

Live the Pillars: Reflect on which of the Seven Pillars resonates most with you today. How can you practice that quality more intentionally this week?

"Becoming a servant leader is not a destination, it's a lifelong practice. Each choice made in love brings us one step closer to living the kind of legacy Biscuit left behind."

Concluding Chapter

Servant Leadership in Life: Biscuit's Enduring Lessons

"What we have once enjoyed we can never lose;
all that we love deeply becomes a part of us."
— Helen Keller

Throughout this book, I have reflected on people who lived these principles, but Biscuit taught me that the deepest lessons of servant leadership often come through the relationships closest to our hearts.

Some lives leave footprints so soft we do not notice their depth until long after they are gone. Biscuit's life was like that. Her presence was quiet, tender, joyful, and yet its impact has echoed far beyond the years we shared with her. It continues in the way we listen to one another, in how we approach life's challenges, and in how we choose to lead with love rather than authority.

When I look back, I see that Biscuit was teaching us the lessons of servant leadership long before I knew to name them. She taught us to show up for others, to listen with the heart, and to lend strength without demanding attention. She reminded us that leadership is not a title or role, it is a way of being, a posture of humility, grounded in love.

While I worked through the challenges of public service and community life, Biscuit shared her wisdom through action rather than instruction. She seemed to understand that true leadership begins at home, among those entrusted to our care. It is tested most in ordinary moments: at the kitchen table, on a late-night walk, or greeting a child after a tough day.

In time, I came to understand that the lessons Biscuit taught at home became the foundation of how I built trust at work. People responded to sincerity. They recognized when they were heard. They thrived when they were valued. And together, we could do far more than anyone could do alone.

Biscuit reminded us to find joy even in difficult seasons. She showed us that play is not a distraction from responsibility, it is often a doorway to healing. Even as she aged and her steps slowed, her enthusiasm never faded. She lived with gratitude. Every day, she seemed to whisper, *This moment is a gift. Let's enjoy it together.*

As her final days approached, we saw a new depth to her leadership. As her body weakened, her spirit remained strong. She continued to greet us, to offer comfort, and to stay close, a reminder that love does not retreat in hardship. Her courage taught us that service is not about strength, it is about presence. She gave all she had until the very end.

When we said goodbye, our family felt the weight of her absence. Yet over time, sadness softened into gratitude. We began to understand that losing her was not the end of her story, it was the beginning of her legacy. Her lessons continued to guide us, shaping how we lived, loved, and led. In ways seen and unseen, she remained by our side.

Biscuit taught us that servant leadership is not reserved for special occasions. It is practiced daily, in kindness, patience, and small acts of courage. It thrives when we listen without judgment, when we offer hope without expectation, and when we lead through compassion rather than control. Her life was a testament to the power of humble service.

As the years have passed, her presence has never faded. I still feel her walking beside me, nudging me forward, reminding me to notice the needs of others. Her lessons accompany me in new places, with new people, helping me greet each day with an open heart. Her spirit continues to whisper: *Slow down. Listen. Serve with love.*

Her story has become part of our family's story, and now, part of yours. My hope is that through these pages, you have felt her warmth and witnessed the beauty of a life lived in service. May her example encourage you to look for opportunities to lead with compassion wherever you are: at home, at work, and in your community.

When we choose to serve, we carry forward the best parts of those who taught us how. And in doing so, we become part of their enduring legacy.

Personal Reflection

As I stand at this point in my life and look back on the journey Biscuit and I shared, I find myself returning to her lessons with a deeper understanding than ever before. Her gift was never just in what she did, but in who she was. Through her quiet devotion and steady presence, she taught me that servant leadership is not a technique or a strategy, it is a way of living. It is a posture of the heart. It comes to life in the smallest expressions of compassion, patience, and loyalty. Biscuit lived those truths every day, long before I could name them.

There are moments when I still picture her trotting ahead on the path, looking back to make sure we were close behind. She never rushed us, she simply encouraged us to keep going. Her gentle glances reminded me that leadership is not about dragging others forward, it is about walking with them. Even now, I feel her presence guiding me with that same quiet confidence.

As I continue to grow as a servant leader, I've learned that the work is never done. There is always more to learn, more kindness to offer, more listening to do. The world changes, seasons shift, roles evolve, yet the call to serve remains constant. Biscuit taught me that we never age out of love, compassion, or purpose. Whether young and eager or older and reflective, we are always invited to give what we can.

Her influence has stretched far beyond the years we spent together. It shows up in how I greet others, how I listen, how I choose to respond rather than react. It shows up when I take a walk to clear my mind or when I sit quietly with someone who is struggling, offering presence rather than answers. These small actions, inspired by her example, have become part of who I am. They remind me that we lead best not by directing others, but by serving them.

I've learned, too, that grief is not an ending, it is a transformation. Losing Biscuit was deeply painful, but that pain softened over time into gratitude: gratitude for the years we shared, for the joy she brought us, and for the way she expanded my capacity to love. I used to think legacy meant leaving something behind for people to remember. Biscuit showed me that true legacy is reflected in how we live, how we make others feel, and how we help people become better versions of themselves. Her legacy lives not only in my heart, but in the hearts of those I now have the privilege to serve.

There are still moments when I ask myself, *What would Biscuit do here?* Sometimes the answer is simple: be kind, be patient, and listen. Other times, the answer is harder: be brave, step forward, and offer yourself even when it feels costly.

But always, her example reminds me that every act of service, no matter how small, holds the power to comfort, encourage, and inspire.

As I enter a new chapter of my life, I think about the lessons she taught. I ask myself whether I am leading with compassion, whether I am listening fully, whether I am lifting others up. When I pause long enough to answer honestly, I feel her presence: steady, encouraging, patient. She reminds me that servant leadership is not about who we are on our best day, but about who we strive to be every day.

Wishes for Your Journey

May you walk with an open mind and an open heart.
May you see the quiet places where care is needed,
and have the courage to move toward them.

May you listen with passion, speak gently,
and offer your presence freely.

May humility find its way in your service.
May you be a source of comfort,
a bearer of calmness that offers peace,
and a companion to those who travel with you.

And may the spirit of Biscuit,
the joyful friend, the trustworthy partner,
the gentle guide,
remind you that every act of compassion
is an act of leadership,
and every gift of kindness
carries forward a legacy that never ends.

As you continue your own journey,
may you find moments of light,
reasons for hope,
and people who help you see all that is good.

Walk gently.
And lead with heart.

Guiding Lights: Special Gratitude

Some people enter our lives and quietly change everything. They teach not by instruction, but by example, shaping how we listen, how we serve, and how we lift others.

The individuals honored in this section helped illuminate my own journey into servant leadership. Their presence and guidance are gifts I will carry always. They have left imprints on my heart.

Abe Hassan

I would like to honor my great friend and mentor, Abe Hassan. Abe came to this country from Sudan and, as a young man, faced many challenges to be welcomed and accepted. In time, he devoted his life to creating jobs through Merrick Community Services. He led training programs for disadvantaged people in construction by cultivating environments where they could thrive, no matter their background. He paired his students with jobs, and his work was life-changing for many people.

Abe and I worked together at MnDOT, where he led initiatives to build relationships with communities historically underrepresented in the transportation field. He was a trusted and respected voice in those communities, and when he brought me alongside him to listen and learn, doors opened.

We often stood shoulder to shoulder in rooms where emotions ran high. These conversations could be difficult, even contentious, yet they always ended with mutual respect and a shared sense of purpose. Throughout it all, Abe and I had each other's backs. We shared many serious moments, but also plenty of laughter.

I learned so much simply by being in his presence. Abe lived servant leadership every day, offering compassion, empathy, understanding, and joy to everyone around him. His influence made me a stronger, better leader and human being.

Thank you, Abe, for being part of my life and for showing me what it means to serve with heart.

Shirley McCall

Shirley McCall is one of my earliest mentors and my hero. As a young employee of the Federal Highway Administration, I spent six months on assignment at the Trans Tech (now TransSTEM) Academy at Cardozo High School in Washington, D.C. The school was diverse and vibrant, and the Academy focused on helping students in grades 9–12 explore future careers in transportation.

Shirley, the Academy's Director, led with extraordinary skill and grace. My role was to support her in program development, but truthfully, I was there to learn, and learn I did. Watching Shirley work with teachers and students was witnessing servant leadership in motion.

She saw strength in every student, especially those whose backgrounds presented challenges. She filled gaps with compassion, not judgment. In her office, Shirley kept a rack of professional clothing so students could borrow something to wear to an interview. Her kindness was practical, grounded, and unwavering.

Even though my time with her was short, Shirley shaped my understanding of what leadership could be: quiet, encouraging, and deeply human. At the time, I didn't know the term "servant leadership." I only knew I was watching someone who cared enough to lift others up.

Thank you, Shirley, for your example, your generosity, and for being my hero.

Biscuit the Dog Companion Journal Invitation

A Place to Sit, Reflect, and Lead with Heart

Throughout this book, you've walked alongside Biscuit, through joy, challenge, loss, and the quiet moments of everyday life.

If her story stirred something in you, the journey doesn't end here.

The Biscuit the Dog Companion Journal was created so you have a place to explore what servant leadership looks like in *your* life. Not in theory, not in policy, but in the ordinary moments where presence becomes love, and love becomes leadership.

This journal invites you to:
- Capture the stories that shaped you
  Your first mentors, your quiet teachers, those who stood beside you.
- Notice the moments when you served without expectation
  When you shared time, patience, or encouragement.
- Record the people who trusted you to lead with empathy
  The ones who taught you that compassion is strength.
- Reflect on the seasons of vulnerability and recovery
  When you leaned on others, or when someone sat quietly beside you.
- Discover how love becomes legacy
  In the way we show up, support, protect, and lift others.

Each section of the journal mirrors the chapters of this book, not as homework, but as an open space for conversation between your life and Biscuit's lessons.

Feel free to write paragraphs, short reflections, memories, prayers, drawings, or silent moments of gratitude.

There is no right way to use it. Just begin.

If leadership is truly service, and service is truly love, then the lessons Biscuit lived are not complete until they are lived through you.

Let this journal be a place to slow down, listen deeply, and discover your own servant leadership story, one moment at a time.

Leadership Inspiration

Leadership rarely looks like leadership when we are living it.
It appears in the everyday, through moments so small they are almost
invisible.

It might be the person who listens when everyone else speaks.
The colleague who checks in quietly after a difficult meeting.
The mentor who opens a door and steps aside so someone else can
walk through.
The neighbor who brings comfort without needing a reason.
The friend who shows up again and again, long after the crowd has
moved on.

Over the years, I've met many people who lived this way.
You've met some of them in these pages.
They did not seek recognition or authority.

They led by putting others first,
by bringing hope into places that had forgotten how to hold it,
by serving with humility.

Their lives remind me that servant leadership is not measured in grand
gestures.
It is measured in presence,
in kindness offered without expectation,
in patience given when it would be easier to turn away,
in the courage to care when others choose indifference.

This was Biscuit's way.

She never knew she was leading, she simply loved, listened, and stayed close.

And somehow, through those simple acts, she taught everyone around her how to be better.

Servant leaders rarely announce themselves.

They move quietly, gently, steadily.

They lift others until those others find their own strength.

They mend what is fragile.

They see what is overlooked.

They remind us who we can be at our best.

If there is one truth I carry forward from Biscuit's life, it is this:

Leadership is not what you do for others,

leadership is what others see in themselves because of you.

If you can make someone feel seen,

if you can restore someone's hope,

if you can listen without judgment or lead without claiming credit,

you are already walking the path of a servant leader.

Carry that forward.

The world needs more hearts like yours.

Like Biscuit, lead with a gentle heart, and leave footprints of kindness wherever you walk.

A Final Thought

You don't need to be perfect to lead.

You just need to be present, faithfully, gently, and with an open heart.

Biscuit did it every day.

So can you.

Books and Resources That Inspired This Work

The following books, videos, and teachings helped shape my understanding of servant leadership and informed the reflections shared in this work. They are offered here as resources for readers who wish to explore these ideas more deeply.

- Foundational Servant Leadership
  - Robert K. Greenleaf — *Servant Leadership: A Journey into the Nature of Legitimate Power and Greatness*
  - Don M. Frick & James W. Sipe — *The Seven Pillars of Servant Leadership: Practicing the Wisdom of Leading by Serving*

- Leadership and Personal Growth
  - Stephen R. Covey — *The 7 Habits of Highly Effective People*
  - Stephen M. R. Covey — *The Speed of Trust*
  - Peter Block — *Stewardship*
  - Margaret J. Wheatley — *Leadership and the New Science*
  - Henry O. Dormann — *Letters from Leaders*
  - James Kouzes & Barry Posner — *The Leadership Challenge*
  - Jim Collins — *Good to Great*
  - Kevin and Jackie Freiberg — *NUTS! (The Story of Southwest Airlines)*
  - James Maxwell — *The 21 Indispensable Qualities of a Leader*

- Ken Blanchard & Colleen Barrett — *Leading with LUV*
  - Jacqueline Byrd — *Voice of the Innovator*
  - Joe Torre — *Joe Torre's Ground Rules for Winners*

- Kindness and Community
  - Orly Wahba — *Life Vest Inside: Kindness Boomerang* (Short Video)
  - Lance Wubbels & Mac Anderson — *To a Child, Love Is Spelled T-I-M-E* (Short Video)
  - Juana Bordas — *Salsa, Soul and Spirit*

- Inspiration from the Natural World
  - A variety of animal-inspired reflections, stories, and writings that remind us how often wisdom shows up in simple, everyday moments.